# THE
# Victory
# OF
# Surrender

# THE Victory OF Surrender

## GORDON FERGUSON

One Merrill Street
Woburn, MA 01801
1-800-727-8273   Fax (617) 937-3889

*Cover: Nora Robbins*
*Layout design: Chris Costello and Nora Robbins*

Printed in the United States of America

ISBN 1-884553-64-8

# To Theresa, the love of my life.

In our 30 years of marriage, you have demonstrated the fine art of surrender far better than I have written about it. As we have changed careers, raised children, moved all over the country, and traveled all over the world, you maintained a marvelous sense of humor in the midst of some seriously challenging times. Never have you allowed a negative attitude toward life or people to invade your heart or speech, for your childlike faith never dims. You are a totally unique person and delightful partner.

# CONTENTS

# FOREWORD

When Jesus saw a widow put two small copper coins into the temple poor box, he gathered his disciples and told them she had given more than all the others, for she had given all she had. This instance came shortly before Jesus knew he was to be crucified. If he had gone to his Father's house to prepare for the cross, then perhaps he was taken by the woman's example because in her he saw a kindred spirit. He was about to sacrifice everything, trusting in God to raise him from the dead, just as the woman sacrificed everything, trusting in God to be her comfort. In sacrifice, both Jesus and the widow were comrades in the fellowship of surrender.

For many people the concept of surrender is *anathema*, yet Gordon has again given us an insightful book to help us conquer through the Spirit what the flesh so tries to resist. We so often use the compliment, "His life backs up his message," and in Gordon's case nothing can be more truly said. As elder, evangelist, teacher, father, husband, friend and author, Gordon is a living example of what happens when a man "lets go and lets God." As one who has experienced the thrills and chills of trusting God totally, Gordon now leads us along the path of submission, teaching us that the greatest act of strength anyone will ever accomplish is to bow before our Creator and humbly rely on him.

Take this book not only into your library but into your heart. Join with Jesus and the widow and with every soul who ever put his or her life in God's hands. Join with Gordon as in his own refreshing way he leads you into an experience you may have forgotten or possibly never found at all. Become a comrade in submission, a kindred spirit in the fellowship of surrender.

Steve Johnson
*New York, New York*

# ACKNOWLEDGMENTS

Many have been the influences for good in my life. I am a composite of a number of people. My father instilled the elements of toughness and honesty into my character. As a result, I have been able to hold on to my principles in trying times. My mother gave me my love for children, for people with unusual personalities, and for the Word of God. She has been an outstanding mother to me and grandmother to my children. My wife, Theresa, has given me unconditional love I needed but never deserved. I learned to feel secure in God's love by feeling secure in her love. My children, Bryan and Renee, have provided me with joys which couldn't be spoken and concerns which shouldn't be spoken! As adults, they now bring joy in a different way—the joy of best-friend relationships. You two are awesome. Your choices for God have released me from the "worried dad" stage!

A number of men through the years have taught me much about the subject of surrender, directly and indirectly. Good books have found their way into my views of spirituality and surrender. Many lovers of God have shown me the practical aspects of surrender as they faced the bad times and good times with unquenchable faith. God has shown his patience with me through the patience of those whom he placed in my life at pivotal points. God has made all the difference in my life by providing the people who made all the difference. Through his servants I have been changed for eternity.

Working with the staff of DPI is always a privilege. Tom Jones is an outstanding editor and close personal friend. The editing process between us is never predictable but always fun. He does not hesitate to challenge my thinking and my will. Sheila Jones, Kim Hanson and Jerri Newman offered valuable suggestions as copy editors for this book. They were all secure enough in their skills to speak up when they found areas that needed to be improved. Nora Robbins, in her last project as DPI's art director, did another great job with the cover and interior design. To all of you and others at DPI who made this book possible, God bless you for your help and encouragement!

A special note of thanks to Randy McKean and Jimmy Rogers, who allow me the opportunity to write by giving me great latitude in arranging my ministry schedule. Randy in particular has been the greatest motivator behind my writing and a great contributor of excellent ideas. Also, my thanks go to Scott Leete for helping me several years ago to conquer my computer phobia and finally "boot up." I would have written only a small percentage of my materials had I not joined the technology of the 20th century slightly before we enter the 21st!

Finally, to God be the glory for anything helpful that flows from my heart and pen. He has spent years training me for teaching and writing through unique experiences. He is my Father, my friend, and my life. In the hope of helping others see him more clearly and love him more deeply, I offer this book in the name of his Son, Jesus the Christ.

# INTRODUCTION

L et go and let God! This may sound like a noble little spiritual cliché, but it describes perhaps the most important lesson we will ever learn.

I am reminded of the story of the man who was climbing a mountain, lost his footing and began sliding toward the edge of a great precipice. Just as he went over the edge, he grabbed a little scrub bush and held on for dear life, dangling over empty space. The bush's root system was starting to pull loose from its tenuous hold on the rocky soil. The man began yelling at the top of his lungs, "Help! Help! Is anyone up there who can help me?"

A voice answered, "Yes, I can help you."

Intensely relieved, the man yelled, "Who is it?"

The answer came back, "I'm the Lord."

The man offered his praises and gratitude to God, and then asked, "God, what do you want me to do now?"

The answer came back, "Let go of the bush."

After a long period of silence, the man yelled, "Is anyone else up there?"

Letting go of our own "bushes" in this life is no less challenging. From the time we are born, we want to be in control of our own destiny. We have trouble trusting that others have our best interests in mind or that they have the ability to make the correct decisions about our lives. And the greater the possible consequences of our choices, the more difficult to let another control the decisions and events which affect us. Putting God into the equation does not eliminate the challenge. We may say that God is all-knowing, all-powerful and all-loving, but trusting him at an emotional level is still difficult. Many of us have this subject figured out well enough intellectually, but emotionally we lag far behind.

*Surrender equals victory. Let go and let God.* Simply stated, this concept means that we give up the emotional control of our lives and everything about them. It does not mean that we no longer think or feel or have preferences. But it does mean that we end up facing all decisions with the same heart expressed by Jesus when he said, "Yet not as I will, but as you will." We think and we plan, but we emotionally surrender the final outcome to God. We count the cost by looking at the most extreme possible outcome and then we accept it in advance with our hearts, in case it ends up to be his will. We pray for what we judge is the best solution but are willing to accept the worst scenario if necessary.

Most often we are not faced with having to accept a grievous outcome. God is full of grace. He does not treat us as our sins deserve, and he often delivers us from the object of our fears. He is unquestionably on our side, always having our very best interests on his heart. But only he is God, understanding both our nature and the nature of the spiritual battle. Life is not easy, and it always ends in death. Therefore, we must be prepared to face some intense situations during our sojourn on earth. Only one path is open to us if we desire to please God and live without being consumed by fear and anxiety—*surrender*.

This book is no popular-styled self-help tool. It takes a serious look at developing the kind of faith that will enable you to endure any test that comes your way. As a disciple of Jesus Christ, you will not be shielded from cross bearing. Instead, your confession of him guarantees that you will have spiritual struggles. Self-denial is the very first prerequisite for being his follower. When injustices, illnesses, insults, rejections and emotional pain flood your life, surrender to the will of God is the only way to survive the challenges.

When you can face the worst that Satan can throw at you and surrender it to God, then life takes on new meaning. You can live in another dimension that few ever discover. The Bible clearly says that we can be free of anxiety and full of a peace which defies description (Philippians 4:6-7). If you study the biblical principles found in this book, you will be rewarded beyond—far beyond—your expectations. No subject is more needed and no relief more widely sought than the victory which accompanies true surrender. My prayer is that you will take to heart the concepts of mature faith and drink deeply of its rewards. And may your surrender bring joy to God's heart, glory to his name, and success to his purpose of changing our world. Let the changes begin with us!

PART

I

Surrender:
The Key to
Spiritual Power

# CHAPTER 1

# Surrender:
# Another Word for Faith

T he idea of surrender has long appealed to me as a fundamental aspect of faith. One of the bigger challenges to my faith has been believing *in advance* that God would do great things for me and through me. Yet, Jesus clearly taught in Mark 11:23-24 that we are to pray for mountains to move. Then believing that we have received it (past tense), it will be given to us (future tense). Faith is "being sure of what we hope for and certain of what we do not see," and without this kind of faith, we cannot please God (Hebrews 11:1, 6).

However, the biggest challenge to my faith has been the surrender of my will to God's. To yield control of my life seemed a staggering prospect at times. Although I had read a few books on the subject when I was a younger minister, my personal struggle with surrender intensified when I approached 40. Given that this age is often associated with mid-life crisis, the timing of my most challenging experiences came as no surprise!

At this point, I was a minister without dreams. The failure to help churches grow in the way I read about in the book of Acts had taken a serious toll on my faith. I felt like a complete failure as I watched the years of my youth slip away without my dreams being realized. As Fantine sang in *Les Miserables*, life had "killed the dream I dreamed." During this period, I at least learned to pray for prolonged periods and to be gut-level honest with God. But my inner being was characterized by emotions far different than "the peace of God which transcends all understanding" (Philippians 4:7).

A turning point in my search for peace and purpose came when an acquaintance suggested two books to help in my struggle: *The God Players* by Earl Jabay[1] and *The Rejection Syndrome* by Charles Solomon.[2] I bought both of them at once and started reading Jabay's. This book exposes our desire to be the god of our own lives. I can still remember reading it in an airplane awaiting takeoff from the Denver airport during a snowstorm. As the deicing truck was doing its job, the people seated around me were anxious about the buildup of snow on the wings and the possible threat to our safety. However, my only concern was my grievous sin of being a "god-player." For probably the first time, I realized the shallowness of my surrender, and therefore, my lack of faith. The conviction of that hour remains vivid in my mind, even after more than a dozen years.

After returning home, I began to pray earnestly about my need and my growing desire to surrender all that I had to God. One morning my prayers reached their zenith, and as I was down on my knees with arms outstretched to heaven, I promised God that I would relinquish everything to him—my future, my health, my life and death, my family, my finances, and anything else important to me that came to mind. After that tearful but exhilarating session, the weight of the world moved off my shoulders and onto the shoulders of God, where it belonged (1 Peter 5:7). What a relief!

But almost immediately, my new-found peace began to be shattered by the not-so-simple cares of life. The events described next sound quite humorous now, but they were far from funny when they occurred. The water pipes in our utility room had been frozen for over a week, and about 5 a.m. on a Sunday

---

[1] Earl Jabay, *The God Players* (Grand Rapids, Michigan: Pyranee Books, Zondervan Publishing House, 1969, 1970, 1987). Currently out of print.

[2] Charles R. Solomon, *The Rejection Syndrome* (Wheaton, Illinois: Tyndale House, 1982). Currently out of print.

morning (Christmas Day), they thawed and began spurting out water in the walls. It sounded like a freight train was running through our house. I finally found a flashlight, the necessary tools and the underground valve in the front yard and shut the water off. Ordinarily, such a rude awakening would have produced some stress, but at that point I was surrendered and at peace. I took this minor inconvenience in stride and began formulating Plan B for my morning.

The church for which I preached had built a new building, and it had a shower in one of the bathrooms. Early that Christmas morning I went to the building, enjoyed a hot shower, and rejoiced that my surrendered life was holding up under adverse circumstances! But the battle had only just begun.

Since Christmas fell on a Sunday that year, I had planned a special service focusing on the entire life of Jesus and concluding with his resurrection. The plan was for me to read a number of passages of Scripture, followed by congregational hymns which related to them. As I started the sermon, I turned to the first passage and began reading it to the congregation. Something seemed amiss, but I kept reading. Finally, it dawned on me that the passage I was reading had absolutely nothing to do with Jesus' life or my lesson! I apologized, figured out my mistake and proceeded to read the correct passage.

Then the song leader announced the first song and started leading it. To say that his leadership of the selected song was "weak" would have been far too kind. He neglected to tell me that he was unfamiliar with most of the songs I had assigned him. Eventually, that first song ended, and I rose to read the second passage of Scripture. Unbelievably, it, too, was the wrong text. I realized this more quickly the second time, but by now my surrender had worn thin. I was exasperated and embarrassed.

After the song leader had butchered his second song, I was wishing that all of this had been a dream. My normal sense of being in control and efficient was giving way to a feeling of chaos. Just when I thought I couldn't get more rattled, a first-time visitor to our church began having a seizure of some kind. After the members with medical training had helped the poor soul, I resumed my sermon. However, I now had a shaky voice and a nervous tic in one of my eyelids. No one in that church had ever witnessed me (or probably any other preacher) in such a state!

Finally, the debacle ended, and I retreated to my home to pray and re-surrender. But my challenges had only begun. I invited a friend over to assess my plumbing problems. Quite a good handyman and builder, he offered some suggestions about fixing not only my immediate problem but about doing some remodeling while we were in the process. It all sounded great to me! I had a good excuse for improving the quality of my home for a minimal cost of both time and money. At least, that was the plan. God, it seemed, had different plans.

The whole project became a nightmare. Nothing went as planned. Older houses have problems lurking underneath the surface, and we uncovered quite a number of such glitches in construction. The amount of time and money exceeded my wildest estimates. My possession possessed me for several months. I couldn't get the project off my mind or out of my bank account. Now my surrender had not simply worn thin—it had disappeared entirely. My emotional state was worse than it had been for months. I was in "survival" mode, trying to outlast this terrible ordeal and wishing that I had never bought such a house in the first place.

During the latter stages of this awful project, I sat in my church office one day wondering how my life had come so unraveled in such a short time. I happened to see a little pamphlet in my desk and glanced at the first page. I discovered that it contained a synopsis of Solomon's book, *The Rejection Syndrome*, explaining how an occasion of surrender was often followed by some serious times of testing. The example mentioned was taken from the life of Jesus. His baptism was followed immediately by the 40 days of temptation in the wilderness—an experience planned and executed by God! "Then Jesus was led by the Spirit into the desert to be tempted by the devil" (Matthew 4:1).

As soon as I read this section, I immediately left the office, went home and started reading the book. Feeling very surrendered and victorious after reading the first book (*The God Players*), I had not even started the second. I now read it nonstop for hours, refusing to go to bed until I had finished it. By the time I went to sleep that night, I could see how my current situation fit into a predictable biblical pattern. Before that day, I had grasped the concept of surrender, but had little understanding of the tests that come with surrender. Since then, I have experienced many victories of surrender, involving far more serious matters than a building project. Aside from my study of the grace of God, no other study has blessed my life more than that of surrender.

The biblical admonition to surrender all that we *have* and *are* to God himself is abundantly clear. Jesus said,

> "If anyone would come after me, he must deny himself and take up his cross and follow me. For whoever wants to save his life will lose it, but whoever loses his life for me and for the gospel will save it" (Mark 8:34-35).

And on another occasion, he declared,

> "I tell you the truth, unless a kernel of wheat falls to the ground and dies, it remains only a single seed. But if it dies, it produces many seeds. The man who loves his life will lose it, while the man who hates his life in this world will keep it for eternal life" (John 12:24-25).

While the Scriptures may be plain on this subject, grasping the concept at the emotional level is not easy—nor is the implementation of the concept in our lives on a daily basis. We are helped with this if we understand that surrender is simply another word for biblical faith. One of the primary definitions of faith is trust—trusting God to do with us and through us what we could never do in our own power. Surrender is a recognition of our total dependence on God, involving a deep trust that relinquishes control to him.

Surrender has much more to do with *attitudes* than with *actions*. God always expects us to do what we can in any situation. He is not interested in doing for us what we can do for ourselves. But he is interested in our relying on him in *everything* we do, recognizing that all opportunities and abilities come from him anyway. Surrender means that we are *God-reliant*, not *self-reliant*.

In order to better identify the concept, a practical illustration might help. The owner of a company and an employee of the same company are both vitally interested in the success of the company. Both are hard workers. However, the owner feels differently about the company. He is almost constantly thinking about it, whether at work or at home. He reads status reports and projections over and over in fear that he may have overlooked something. His life seems to be *controlled* by his concern for the company.

On the other hand, the employee works hard while on the job, but then leaves work behind when his day is over. He may do some preparation at home for the next day, but his mind is relaxed toward his job. He gave it his best effort while he was working, and afterwards there is little else he can do. He simply has recognized what he *can* and *cannot* control. The owner has missed that very important principle. He really feels that everything depends on *his* entrepreneurial prowess.

The Christian has to decide whether he is a "laborer" or an "owner" in this business called *life*. If he is simply a servant of God, he works and lets God do the "worrying." If he is trying to control everything, he is in reality attempting to be the lord of his own life. Such an approach is *faithless* and *fruitless*, yet it is the approach of all Christians at least *some* of the time, and that of some Christians nearly *all* of the time! We surrender, deny ourselves and take up our crosses, only to gradually resume emotional control of our lives. Surrendering is not a once-for-all accomplishment; it is a daily challenge. But with each victory comes a peace inside which is truly beyond comprehension. The victory found in surrender is available to and attainable by all who are determined to gain it and keep it. However, we must understand the spiritual principles involved, along with their practical applications; and we must be fully aware of the challenges that must be faced and conquered to consistently live the surrendered lifestyle.

# CHAPTER 2

# Surrender:
# Against the Grain

J esus Christ came into our world in order to free us from bondage. However, the bondage is far deeper than we imagine. Overt sin is not our most serious problem; it is basically a *symptom* of a far deeper problem. Like Eve in the Garden, we want to be the god of our own lives. Satan knew exactly how to entice her to fall—with a promise that she could be like God.

## Our Nature Rebels Against It

Human nature has not changed since Eve's day. The desire to be in control, especially of our personal lives, is deeply ingrained in our nature. We are clearly threatened by whatever would lessen our control. This remarkably strong *bent* in our personality leads us to become adept manipulators of people and circumstances, and we try the same with God. From infancy, many of our thoughts and energies are channeled toward obtaining and maintaining control. To make matters worse, we usually don't even realize what we are doing, for it truly becomes second nature to us. Selfishness is an incredibly pervasive sin! No wonder Jesus' central requirement for his disciples was to "deny self"!

Jesus has the cure for this dreadful malady of *self*, but few avail themselves of it. Because we do not embrace his program, or will not, we often exchange the bondage of sin for the bondage of a powerless religion. Satan knows that we are easy to fool because God's way looks too painful. To avoid the pain, we often avoid the cross and remain alive to our self-promoting tendencies. We may appear spiritual and act spiritual, yet still be controlled by the old self. Religion without self-denial and continual cross-bearing is useless. Perhaps our consciences are eased temporarily, but eventually the veneer wears off, exposing the inner frustration that fills the soul. When our lives do not change at the character level, we continue to struggle with many of the same problems as people outside of Christ, and others are not attracted to the kingdom by our lives. In all of this, the peace described in Philippians 4:7 remains an elusive mystery to us. If we remain on this course, our experiment with religion is destined to end in failure.

If these frustrations continue for long enough, we are strongly tempted to go back into the world. Some who take this route then claim to be happier. While I once would have argued with their claim, I now do not. They *are* happier. The only burden which is heavier than sin is the yoke of a powerless religion. Attempting to practice a self-propelled Christianity cannot satisfy the soul's deepest needs, nor can it last indefinitely. A religion without a daily crucifixion in the lives of its adherents is, without question, powerless and useless. Either we lose our lives, thereby gaining them; or we hold on to them, thereby losing them (Mark 8:34-35). No compromise can be made on this point. If Jesus is not "Lord of all" in our lives, he is not Lord at all!

Motivating people to surrender is a high priority for God, and he has a number of ways to do it. His first choice is to move us by his love. As Paul put it in Romans 2:4, "Or do you show contempt for the riches of his kindness, tolerance and patience, not realizing that God's kindness leads you toward repentance?" Sending his only Son to die on a cross was the ultimate demonstration of his love and should move us to repent and surrender to the One who loves us so deeply.

Sadly, most of us are not sufficiently moved by the grace of God to surrender long-term. God's grace may motivate us to begin our walk with Jesus, but to move us to the continual surrender he requires usually takes more drastic measures. At certain times in our lives, we become rebellious to the point that deep pain, physical or emotional, is the only thing that will prompt us to re-surrender. As tenaciously as we may hold on to life on a selfish plane, enough misery will make death seem preferable to life. At that point, we are ready to be crucified with Christ once again.

A friend of mine shared with me his experience with an elderly man who had terminal cancer. The first time my friend (his minister) visited him after the diagnosis, the man was terrified at the thought of dying. As the months wore on, the old gentleman wasted away incredibly. He looked like a skeleton covered with skin. His heart and kidneys, however, were quite strong and simply would not give in to death, at least not for a long time. My friend's final visit with him was quite different from that first visit. The dying man tried to speak, but his voice was barely audible, and my friend could not understand. He then motioned for my friend to put his ear down near his mouth. He posed only this question: "Why can't I die?" His suffering was so great that his fear of death was totally obliterated by the pain of life. Now death seemed a welcome friend.

Are not we spiritually sometimes just like that suffering man? We fight God for control, and we fight to the point that we question God's wisdom, power and even his love! But he loves us enough to increase the pressure in order to bring us to our senses. We may weep and wail in self-pity, begging for the cup of suffering to pass, but God has only one program for those who would follow his Son—total, unconditional surrender. The *Via Dolorosa* remains forever the only way back to God. Most of our crises are designed to produce our surrender and subsequent growth. Even Jesus was perfected for his task of serving through suffering (Hebrews 5:8-9). We need not imagine that we will be matured without it (Hebrews 12:5-11; James 1:2-3). It is through many hardships that we enter the heavenly kingdom (Acts 14:22); and many of these hardships come about because we refuse to stay surrendered, and must once again be taught the futility of self-reliance. If we are hard-headed and hard-hearted, we may renew our efforts to pull ourselves up by our own bootstraps. In this case, most of our "solutions" only prolong the battle and block our way to true freedom.

We human beings are our own worst enemies. We want control. We want our own judgment, our own opinions, our own desires, our own power! When we refuse to deny self daily and stay surrendered, a downward cycle of failure, frustration and anger is inevitable. Much of this frustration and anger is actually directed at God, though we may not realize it. We may blame him for not answering our prayers in the way we think he should. Truthfully, our prayers are often little more than requests for God to rubber-stamp our selfish desires. Were we suddenly enabled to see our selfishness as clearly as God does, the shock would be unimaginable! Yes, surrender unquestionably goes against the grain of our basic nature, and openly or subtly, we are very prone to rebel against it.

## Our Culture Rejects It

Just about everything in our culture is set in opposition to anything which even resembles surrender. "Never give in and never give up" is the order of the day! Whereas God's plan to bless man is based on our recognition of our lack of goodness and power, the world's plan is the very opposite. We are not taught to be honest about who we are or to admit who we are not. We are trained to be performers at all costs, and this training promotes a host of spiritually unsavory qualities in us: self-reliance, pride, self-deception and deception of others.

Many years ago, I had the opportunity to speak with a group of college exchange students from Mainland China about religion. They had only a basic knowledge of religion in general and no knowledge of Christianity. Just where would you start a discussion with people with their background? I began with an explanation of the basic goal of all religions—to be good and to do good. However, Christianity approaches this goal from a direction opposite of all other religions. God bluntly informs us that we are not good and do not have the power to do good. If we are willing to agree with God on this point, we can then deny self, become Christians by accepting his grace and receive from him the power to be good and to do good. (Keep in mind that this "being" and "doing" is a relative matter, for our sinful natures are still present. We may seem good when compared to other humans, but compared to God, none of us has any reason to boast.) Consider the following biblical teachings:

*All of us have become like one who is unclean, and all our righteousness acts are like filthy rags (Isaiah 64:6).*

*I know, O LORD, that a man's life is not his own; it is not for man to direct his steps (Jeremiah 10:23).*

*The heart is deceitful above all things
   and beyond cure (Jeremiah 17:9).*

*"If a man remains in me and I in him, he will bear much fruit; apart from me you can do nothing" (John 15:5).*

*I know that nothing good lives in me, that is, in my sinful nature (Romans 7:18).*

A careful reading of the exact wording of these passages tests even the view we Bible believers have of ourselves. Our righteousness is like a menstrual cloth (literal meaning in Hebrew of Isaiah 64:6); not one of us can direct his own steps; our hearts are amazingly deceitful; apart from Jesus, none of us can do anything worthwhile; and nothing good lives in us! Even on the days when we are hitting on all cylinders and obeying God quite well, we are still to admit that we are unworthy servants at best, and have only done our duty (Luke 17:10). What we do well is due to the power of God, and what we do badly is due to our own sinful inclinations. That, my friends, is the evaluation of the very One who designed us and knows us far better than we will ever know ourselves! In all honesty, those descriptions go against our grain, they grate against the views of our proud and arrogant society.

It is not surprising that we, as sinners, have difficulty recognizing and admitting that we are powerless to change and remain changed without God's help. The difficulty notwithstanding, unless we admit this, time will take its toll, and life will reduce us to disappointed cynics. Read any major newspaper, from the front page to the sports page, and you will see that modern man has become separated from the principles of the Bible and blinded to his own lack of goodness without God's grace. Cynicism and pessimism abound. Man is continually looking for ways to compensate for his weakness, rather than admitting the obvious and surrendering to his Maker.

## Think Your Way Out of Your Problems

Many years ago, I attended a PMA (Positive Mental Attitude) *Rally* along with thousands of others. Well-known men and women were assuring us that we could all start thinking in a visionary manner and become wonderful successes in nearly any endeavor we chose. They all told a story of how they, in essence, had pulled themselves up by their own power and determination. In the world's eyes, they were undoubtedly successful. They had become rich and famous in the business world (or at least rich and famous *at the expense* of the business world, since their present occupation was mainly motivational speaking!).

Some of the people on the program had a religious orientation and used enough Scripture quotes to make their thesis sound both feasible and spiritual. For example, Philippians 4:13 was used as *proof-positive* that we could indeed do "everything" through Christ but the *everything* they described seemed to be suspiciously connected to finances and possessions. The passage reads: "I can do everything through him who gives me strength." The context of the passage has nothing to do with materialism and everything to do with surrender to God. Look at the two verses prior to verse 13:

> ...I have learned to be content whatever the circumstances. I know what it is to be in need, and I know what it is to have plenty. I have learned the secret of being content in any and every situation, whether well fed or hungry, whether living in plenty or in want.

Paul had learned through the "University of Hard Knocks" how to be content through surrender *in spite of* the circumstances. Neither his philosophy nor lifestyle would have garnered him a place to speak at that rally. Likely he could not have afforded the entrance fee.

And what shall we say of Jesus? He was an abject failure in the eyes of the world of his day and would be seen in a worse light in our current society. He owned nearly nothing and appeared alarmingly disinterested in possessions. Surely he would have been totally out of place at our little "All the way with PMA" rally!

One ingredient missing from that particular event was the opportunity to examine the bigger picture of the speakers' lives: their marriages, their children or any other criteria of success in the overall business of life. My experience with people from all walks of life suggests that a look behind the scenes would have shown that they were not all that happy when sitting in a dark hotel room contemplating their destiny in time and eternity. Many of the positive-thinking promoters appear to be trying as hard to convince *themselves* as they are others. As I listen to the self-promoters, I am often reminded of the story about the speaker who supposedly wrote in the margin of his notes, "Shout loud—weak point!"

But let's give these promotional professionals the benefit of the doubt. Let's assume that they are well-rounded, well-adjusted human beings who have found the secrets of a happy life. What percentage of people in our society have any chance of imitating the PMA gurus? The large majority of us come from dysfunctional homes, and the percentage of emotionally unbalanced and maladjusted individuals in our midst is growing at a substantial rate. The only ones who seem to be able to really benefit from the self-propulsion ministry are the small minority of already well-adjusted, capable people who do not have the habitual self-defeating behaviors typical of people with dysfunctional backgrounds. The PMA promoters appear to be saying: "Why don't you just become like me? Imitate me, do right and be successful." What they are actually implying is more like this: "Why didn't you have my inborn abilities, my parents, my circumstances and my opportunities? Why aren't you *me?*"

## Paralysis by Psychoanalysis

Let's move the spotlight to another arena in which humanism reigns supreme, namely that of psychology and psychiatry. At the outset, some clarification is in order. I am not at all opposed to true Christian counseling by trained professionals. However, there is a dearth of such help actually available. Many of those who claim to be biblical in their orientation are not. They are more like Freud than Jesus in their approach to helping people. Even those who would build their role as counselor on the Christian foundation still need help from experienced ministry people to sort through the good and bad of their psychological education. When they have mastered the biblical basis for helping people, along with their professional training, then they are in a position to make some valuable contributions.

The "one another" directions in the New Testament (NT) are God's design for us to help each other. Paul's view stated in Romans 15:14 must become our view: "I myself am convinced, my brothers, that you yourselves are full of goodness, complete in knowledge and competent to instruct one another." The bulk of our counseling needs can and should be taken care of in our relationships in the body of Christ, the church. The more difficult cases can be handled by ministry staff, and the truly challenging situations by a Christian counselor.

Professional counseling is not a cure-all for the ills of our society. We have more counseling available than ever before, and yet our population is virtually saturated with people who have crippling emotional problems. The humanistic approach to counseling is not curing our ills. Some individuals may be helped in some ways to cope and function in the world; however, herein lies the real problem. God intends for the consequences of sins (whether *against* us or *by* us) to bring us to our knees, and cause us to look up to him for help. But just when an individual reaches that point, he then is all too often taught to *cope* rather than *break* before God. Even the word "break" sounds threatening to us, and yet consider the words of David in Psalm 51:17: "The sacrifices of God are a broken spirit; a broken and contrite heart, O God, you will not despise."

In Matthew 21:44, Jesus stated: "He who falls on this stone will be broken to pieces, but he on whom it falls will be crushed." In other words, we all have a choice. Either we choose spiritual brokenness at our own hand (bringing about repentance, surrender, and new life), or we will be crushed by the burdens that life places on our shoulders. These burdens may be those produced by our own sins, those common to all men, or perhaps those brought about directly by God. In the latter case, he is lovingly trying to break us in order that he might really bless us.

At this point, what we need is to bow our knees before the throne of God and turn our crushing burdens over to him (1 Peter 5:7). What we decidedly do *not* need is to be taught how to *cope!* A bottle of tranquilizers only prolongs the suffering. We must begin to look at our lives spiritually and find out what God is trying to teach us. Even if we are facing some tragedy which has nothing to do with our own sins, God still has a plan to use the situation to make us more like his Son. (See Romans 8:28-29.)

It is vital to understand that the basic function of psychology is *diagnosis*. Trained professionals can help individuals to explore their past and learn something about the influences which shaped their lives. But knowing how we got emotionally damaged does not make the damage disappear any more than a physician's diagnosis makes our illness go away. I recall one Christian who sought counseling from a professional who did not have a biblical perspective. She quickly learned how much of her emotional struggles tied in with the treatment she had received as a child from her father. She then learned to hate her father in a way that she had not known before. In fact, she loved to hate and lived to hate. She soon withdrew from the God who "allowed" the mistreatment to happen and from the church who could have helped her. To say that her life is now ruled by bitterness would be an understatement.

All of us have scars from our past. The real issue is how we view and use the past. We can realize how needy we are and seek God, or we can accept a humanistic answer. Knowing how you got your "hang-ups" will do little to change them. Looking for the *hand* of God and the *will* of God in the situation will do everything to help *you* change. The real issue is neither how to change the past (too late for that one) nor how to change your present circumstances (many are not changeable). The issue is how to change yourself and how to allow both your past and present circumstances to bring about surrender to God and ongoing growth.

# CHAPTER 3

# Surrender:
# The Paradoxical Way of God

The Scriptures are replete with paradoxical principles. God's wisdom is absolutely opposite the normal thinking processes of men. Strength comes through weakness. Life comes through death. Victory comes through surrender. But voluntary surrender is not easy. Crosses are neither comfortable nor enjoyable. However, Christ cannot be formed in us until we are crucified with him (Galatians 2:20, 4:19).

Surrender, or death to the selfish *self*, is an emotional break from having to be in control. We become willing to yield our lives, our health, our families, our finances, our futures and our plans totally to him. We are willing to accept what we *need* rather than to stubbornly insist on what we *want*. In essence, we allow God to *be* God in our daily lives. We are bound in order to be freed and freed in order to be bound. Amazingly, real life follows as a great calmness pervades our entire being, otherwise known as the "peace which transcends all understanding" (Philippians 4:7). *Crucifixion* gives way to *resurrection!* However, living a resurrected life is living a crucified life. The paradox continues.

In the early days of Israel's history, God was teaching his people the paradoxical principle of surrender. Later the NT writers (like Paul in 1 Corinthians 10) will refer to those days and the lessons they taught. By taking a closer look at the beginning days of Israel as a nation, we can learn much about the subject of surrender and how committed to the principle our God really is. He is *relentless* in his insistence that our lives be based on a faith which surrenders to him.

## The Reality of Bondage

At one time, I used this analogy to describe the earthly sojourn of Christians: The nation of Israel was in Egyptian bondage, and we are in bondage to sin; they were baptized in the Red Sea, and we are baptized into Christ; they then wandered in the wilderness, and we are pilgrims on the earth; they went through the Jordan into the promised land, and we go through death into heaven. However, somewhere along the line through my reading and study, I came across a more accurate and helpful idea.

The story begins with Jacob's family in Egypt, but not in bondage. They did not start off in slavery, nor do we begin our life in the slavery of sin. As Solomon put it in Ecclesiastes 7:29, "This only have I found: God made mankind upright, but men have gone in search of many schemes." However, just as the Israelites were then pressed into slavery (Exodus 1:6-14), our bondage to sin and sorrow begins when we choose rebellion against the will of God. The nature of their bondage worsened as time passed, which aptly describes the progressive effects of our own sins.

Eventually the "sin now, pay later" rule begins to take its toll. Satan's approach is remarkably similar to the basis of our modern credit system. We are encouraged to buy now and pay later, prompting us to pull out the plastic and charge it. After all, we owe it to ourselves, don't we? The problem is that the interest comes due, and it is not cheap. With sin, the interest is higher than we ever thought in its effects on our hearts and lives. On the other hand, God's approach is to pay up front, as in earning money and paying cash. Afterwards, both time and eternity are filled with marvelous spiritual dividends!

Our tendency to focus on accomplishments, education, possessions, pleasure and power is doomed to failure. All of these are dead-end streets. We spend years climbing the ladder of success, only to discover that the ladder is leaning against the wrong wall. The great American Dream of materialistic success turns out to be more like a nightmare. At best, we spend years searching for things that do not ultimately satisfy; at worst, we end up with damaged families, divorces and personal emotional upheaval. These worldly pursuits will not bring lasting satisfaction and happiness, and we end up in bondage, spiritually and emotionally. The writer of Ecclesiastes pursued all of these things, ending up with this analysis: "I have seen all the things that are done under the sun; all of them are meaningless, a chasing after the wind" (Ecclesiastes 1:14).

In the case of Israel, God introduced a plan to deliver them from their bondage. Exodus 3:7-10 describes the plan thus:

> The LORD said, "I have indeed seen the misery of my people in Egypt. I have heard them crying out because of their slave drivers, and I am concerned about their suffering. So I have come down to rescue them from the hand of the Egyptians and to bring them up out of that land into a good and spacious land, a land flowing with milk and honey—the home of the Canaanites, Hittites, Amorites, Perizzites, Hivites and Jebusites. And now the cry of the Israelites has reached me, and I have seen the way the Egyptians are oppressing them. So now, go. I am sending you to Pharaoh to bring my people the Israelites out of Egypt."

Note the parallels to God's plan for us through his Son. He was concerned enough about our plight of slavery in sin to become a man and die for our sins. He longs to lead us into the promised land flowing with spiritual milk and honey, the abundant life in Christ. He has sent Jesus to lead us out of slavery, and he has provided many human leaders to assist us in escaping the ravages of sin.

Our initial understanding of grace makes a serious impact on our hearts, as may be seen in the case of the Israelites in Exodus 4:29-31:

> Moses and Aaron brought together all the elders of the Israelites, and Aaron told them everything the LORD had said to Moses. He also performed the signs before the people, and they believed. And when they heard that the LORD was concerned about them and had seen their misery, they bowed down and worshipped.

They were quite elated, but at this point, they did not yet understand the price to be paid.

As wonderful as the gracious offers of God may sound originally, escaping bondage is not easy. Pharaoh did not turn loose easily or quickly (Exodus 5:1, 4-9). When he upped the ante, demanding the same output of bricks without providing the straw, the people began to have second thoughts. The price was becoming obvious, and it did not coincide with their preconceived ideas about how God would deliver them! They had been in ecstasy contemplating deliverance, but now they were in agony. Predictably, they turned against the leader who first brought God's plan to their attention:

> When they left Pharaoh, they found Moses and Aaron waiting to meet them, and they said, "May the LORD look upon you and judge you! You have made us a stench to Pharaoh and his officials and have put a sword in their hand to kill us" (Exodus 5:20-21).

Even when the deliverance began taking shape after the 10 plagues, they had second thoughts. The notable miracles only had a short-term effect on their thinking. Exodus 14:10-12 describes their faithlessness in these words:

> As Pharaoh approached, the Israelites looked up, and there were the Egyptians, marching after them. They were terrified and cried out to the LORD. They said to Moses, "Was

> it because there were no graves in Egypt that you brought us to
> the desert to die? What have you done to us by bringing us
> out of Egypt? Didn't we say to you in Egypt, 'Leave us alone;
> let us serve the Egyptians'? It would have been better for us to
> serve the Egyptians than to die in the desert!"

We are much like the Israelites. Our victories are often followed by valleys of despair. Circumstances affect us far more profoundly than they should, causing our focus to shift from the power and goodness of God to our own immediate situations. Therefore, we should not be surprised that Jesus gave a clear call for cost counting. The entire book of Luke focuses on the need for repentance, which demands first counting the cost. Luke 14:25-33 is abundantly clear—becoming a follower of Jesus cannot be done on a whim or an emotional high. The price is not inexpensive, for it requires all that we have and are. And you can be sure that Satan will muddy the waters before we make that final decision to submit to Jesus' lordship.

The Israelites did not escape Egypt easily, nor do we escape darkness easily. Initially, we respond with elation to the plan of God, but our flesh is strong. Sin may have its negative consequences, and the darkness may be foreboding, but at least self is still in control and the surroundings are familiar. Step-by-step we work our way through the exodus from sin's slavery, and were it not for the constant intervention of a patient God, none of us would make it out. Praise God that he is persistent in his pursuit of us and determined to save us! By his grace, the Israelites made it out of Egypt, and by that same grace, we are able to make it out of darkness and into his marvelous light.

## The Joy of Deliverance

In the end, Israel escaped only by deciding to place themselves totally in God's hands. God always seems to work it out that our backs are against the wall, and nothing will bring deliverance except his power. He never ceases to bring us to the decision points which make surrender or denial the only real possibilities. Notice what happened at the banks of the Red Sea:

> Moses answered the people, 'Do not be afraid. Stand firm and you will see the deliverance the LORD will bring you today. The Egyptians you see today you will never see again. The LORD will fight for you; you need only to be still'" (Exodus 14:13-14).

Once they made the decision to place their lives totally in God's care and keeping, amazing miracles that produced an unbelievable victory ensued. Exodus 14:29-31 describes their deliverance in these words:

> But the Israelites went through the sea on dry ground, with a wall of water on their right and on their left. That day the LORD saved Israel from the hands of the Egyptians, and Israel saw the Egyptians lying dead on the shore. And when the Israelites saw the great power the LORD displayed against the Egyptians, the people feared the LORD and put their trust in him and in Moses his servant.

This deliverance was followed immediately by a time of mountain-top rejoicing. Exodus 15 describes their singing, dancing and praising of Almighty God. All of their fears and frustrations were ended, and the promises of God embraced. Surely a fairy tale ending to the story would be expected!

In a similar way, we make it through the struggles of cost-counting and accept the plan of God for our deliverance. What a time of rejoicing! The joy of that initial salvation is better felt than described. Once we grasp that all of our sins have been washed away in the blood of Christ, we are on the mountaintop with Jesus. That first night after we become Christians, we either sleep like a baby, or we cannot sleep at all. The Philippian jailer and his family were baptized well after midnight, but they immediately set the table and enjoyed a celebration meal together with Paul and Silas (Acts 16:25-34). Celebrating with great joy is the inevitable response to such a complete deliverance.

However, unless faith and repentance are very strong, fear and negativism can set in quickly. Then we begin to look back at our previous life in a slanted way, imagining it to be much better than it actually was. After Israel had been out of Egypt less than two months, they forgot God's grace and began losing faith.

> *In the desert the whole community grumbled against Moses and Aaron. The Israelites said to them, "If only we had died by the LORD's hand in Egypt! There we sat around pots of meat and ate all the food we wanted, but you have brought us out into this desert to starve this entire assembly to death"* (Exodus 16:2-3).

First, they grumbled about food. God provided manna. Next, they complained about the lack of water in one of their campgrounds, and God provided water out of a rock (Exodus 17:1-7). Then, they complained about not having meat, and God sent hordes of quail (along with a plague; he was losing patience! —Numbers 11:10-34).

We could give more examples, but the point is that in spite of repeated, amazing blessings from God, we humans quickly forget the good when something bad arrives. It is easy to marvel at the Israelites' lack of faith, but are we really different? God gave his Son to die on a cross for our sins. And he made this promise in Romans 8:32: "He who did not spare his own Son, but gave him up for us all—how will he not also, along with him, graciously give us all things?"

Our problem is that the "all things" God stands ready to give are not necessarily the "all things" we have on our minds. As James put it, "When you ask, you do not receive, because you ask with wrong motives, that you may spend what you get on your pleasures" (James 4:3). In other words, we want material things or even spiritual things for selfish reasons. And when

God doesn't rubber-stamp our prayers, we often begin to question him. Our questioning may quickly move to disappointment, frustration, anger and serious loss of faith. And yet God is willing and able to give us *all things!*

In fact, he promised to take all things, good and bad, and work them together for our good (Romans 8:28). In 1 Corinthians 3:21, Paul says that he has already given us all things, and in 2 Corinthians 9:8, he sheds more light on these available blessings with these words: "And God is able to make all grace abound to you, so that in all things at all times, having all that you need, you will abound in every good work." We must see that God's purpose for us is not simply that we be fulfilled and happy from a humanistic perspective. He wants us to be like his Son, and he wants us to abound in the only work that will affect eternity. I have a sentence written in the front of my Bible that captures the essence of this thrust. It simply says, "Never give up your life for anything that death can take away!"

However, like the Israelites, we focus on the relatively insignificant things of this life. When things don't fall into place the way we think they should, we lose our joy and start on the downward spiral into faithlessness. That spiral always begins with a loss of gratitude for what God has already done. The Gentile world of Paul's day began their horrible slide into excess wickedness in exactly this manner:

> *For although they knew God, they neither glorified him as God nor gave thanks to him, but their thinking became futile and their foolish hearts were darkened (Romans 1:21).*

Addressing Christians, Peter wrote:

> *For if you possess these qualities in increasing measure, they will keep you from being ineffective and unproductive in your knowledge of our Lord Jesus Christ. But if anyone does not have them, he is nearsighted and blind, and has forgotten that he has been cleansed from his past sins (2 Peter 1:8-9).*

Ingratitude is a terrible sin. We may have dozens of obvious blessings, but we focus on the one or two things which don't meet with our approval. We then say (or think) many foolish and childish things. "If God would give me this one thing, then I could be really happy." "If God really loved me, he would give me this request." "God's Word doesn't seem to work for me." "I would never treat my child the way God is treating me." On and on we go and crawl into our cocoon of self-absorption, forgetting the countless blessings God has already given us; letting some little unreached goal or blessing *not* received cause us to discount the world's greatest blessing possible—the gift of a crucified Christ and the forgiveness brought about by that awful sacrifice! "But if God would just give me this...." How shameful! How embarrassing! How utterly ungrateful!

When you look at the infantile behavior of the Israelites, do not be smug in your self-righteousness and think to yourself that you would never do such a thing! You have done it many times in one form or another—outwardly and obviously, or inwardly and secretly. But you have done it and so have I. All the more reason to take this business of surrender seriously. When we allow God to be our God, we are at peace with him and our own world. Criticalness and ingratitude go out the window, and appreciation and humility come in. It is time to give up and to grow up! Let's get the deep convictions we need; let's repent, surrender and be filled with inexpressible joy (1 Peter 1:8), thus bringing joy to our Father!

## From Bondage to Bondage

After the Israelites had been delivered from slavery in Egypt, they needed some teaching and training in righteousness. All newcomers to God's kingdom need some follow-up studies to ground them in the faith. At Mt. Sinai, God gave the new nation instructions needed for their life with him. After about a year, he felt they were ready to enter into their new land of milk and honey. At Kadesh Barnea, the twelve spies were sent to spy out the land in preparation for their conquest of it. Sadly, 10 of the spies came back totally humanistic—they saw the bounty of the land, but not the God of the land.

Even after having witnessed nearly two years of fantastic miracles by the Lord, they became faithless. Numbers 13:33 sums it up with this telling observation: "We saw the Nephilim there (the descendants of Anak come from the Nephilim). We seemed like grasshoppers in our own eyes, and we looked the same to them." But again, are we really so different? God has done amazing miracles in our lives. We have viewed his mighty arm in numerous situations, not the least of which was when he emptied that tomb in Jerusalem early one Sunday morning! However, how often do we feel like grasshoppers when we stand in the company of worldly pagans? How often does our conflict-avoiding, people-pleasing nature cause us to avoid confronting the sins in the lives of other Christians, even though God's word is clear on our responsibilities in this area?

When we are unsurrendered, self is in control and we seem as grasshoppers to ourselves and to others. When we are surrendered, God is in control of us, and we become his instruments for the accomplishment of his tasks. The issue is surrender—no question about it. Scripture could not be plainer: "For God did not give us a spirit of timidity, but a spirit of power, of love and of self-discipline" (2 Timothy 1:7). Just where does that spirit of fearfulness come from? Not God! It comes from Satan when he is at the controls of our lives—and we are unsurrendered. God is in control only when we are righteous, and then the grasshopper complex goes out the door. Proverbs 28:1 hits the nail right on the head with these words: "The wicked man flees though no one pursues, but the righteous are as bold as a lion."

Ultimately, the Israelite nation rejected true freedom because most of them lacked faith. They would not have been consigned to the wilderness if they had been surrendered. That was not the original plan of their God. Nor is wandering around in desolate places the plan of God for us. Life does not have to be like a wilderness that we must endure with set jaws until finally we cross the "Jordan River" of death! No special premiums are attached to living a life of struggles at our own hands. Struggle we must, but let it be at the hand of the world because of righteousness, and not because of our own choice to remain unsurrendered. When we do endure the hardships with the right kind of faith, they produce in us a joy and a determination to keep on fighting.

Suffering takes on a different meaning to those who are crucified with Christ:

> The apostles left the Sanhedrin, rejoicing because they had been counted worthy of suffering disgrace for the Name (Acts 5:41).

> Consider it pure joy, my brothers, whenever you face trials of many kinds, because you know that the testing of your faith develops perseverance. Perseverance must finish its work so that you may be mature and complete, not lacking anything (James 1:2-4).

Remain in control, and you lose control of all that matters. Lose control, and you gain control of all that matters. Life with Jesus may be a paradox, but remaining in the bondage of sin and wandering in the wilderness is not paradoxical—it is a vote for misery!

## Finally, FAITH!

The 40 years of wilderness wandering for Israel was both punishment for unbelief and preparation for faith. After the people came to a full realization of the consequences of their faithlessness at Kadesh Barnea, they still took matters into their own hands. Even though God had already pronounced their 40-year sentence and killed the unfaithful spies with a plague, the people tried to invade the land and were soundly defeated (Numbers 14:36-45). Sorrowful they were; repentant they were not. The message of the Bible is unwavering in its demand that we rely completely on God rather than on ourselves.

The next opportunity the Israelites had to enter the promised land, they approached it with a different attitude. Forty years of recurrent attendance at the funerals of unbelieving relatives and friends had made a deep impression. Like the old priest in the movie *Rudy*, they had finally figured out the basics. The movie priest told Rudy something to this effect: "Son, I have lived a long time, and I have learned two very important things about life. One, there is a God; and two, I am not him!"

On the banks of the swollen Jordan River, we find this new generation of Israelites ready to trust and follow God. Similar to a scene four decades earlier, the waters were miraculously parted, and the nation walked through on dry land. Once near Jericho, spies were again sent out, but this time they came back in faith. Just to make sure the people understood that the battle was not to the strong and the race to the swift, the first city was conquered in a most unusual way. They marched around it 13 times over a period of seven days, blew trumpets and shouted. Then God kept his word, giving them the city:

> When the trumpets sounded, the people shouted, and at the sound of the trumpet, when the people gave a loud shout, the wall collapsed; so every man charged straight in, and they took the city (Joshua 6:20).

Can you imagine just how foolish any humanistic person would have felt in that entourage? Walking around a city and then going back to their tents—for six straight days. One would be hard pressed to find that procedure outlined in a battle manual.

Then how would they have felt if the walls had not fallen? The word *foolish* is not in the ballpark! We are tempted to take the story and its outcome for granted, since our hindsight is always 20/20. But truthfully, we feel foolish doing many things in the name of God which are not nearly as ludicrous in appearance as their actions.

Their faith was at a peak, and they were rewarded as a result. But the development of that faith was a drawn-out affair. Total surrender by any person must ultimately stand the tests of God within the test of time. It is paradoxical how something this powerful can be so simple to conceive and yet so difficult to practice. However, its fruits are valuable enough to engage us for a lifetime. Free in slavery and a slave for freedom. Crucified with Christ and alive with him forevermore. Dead and alive, both at once. Surrendered, but always victorious—the paradoxical way of God, to God and for God!

# CHAPTER 4

# Surrender:
# The Only Path to Security

Security is not difficult to obtain when you are a small child. A thunderstorm may wake you up and be terrifying while you are in your own bed, but jumping in between Mom and Dad makes the terror vanish. For some reason, it never occurs to you at that age that lightning could strike *their* room.

As we age, security becomes increasingly difficult to gain and maintain. The more we know about the world in which we live and about ourselves, the more we realize how tenuous life on this planet really is.

Of course, God is the solution for our insecurities and fears. His word outlines these solutions quite clearly. The difficulty is in *application*, not understanding. "Let go and let God!" "The Lord will fight for you; you need only to be still." "Surrender the burdens to God and he will take care of you." "Cast all of your anxiety on him, for he cares for you." What may sound like pat answers are nonetheless true. When will he take away your burdens and anxieties? Just as soon as you give them to him—at the precise moment you truly surrender before his throne.

*Life is tough and then you die.* I have read that statement on bumper stickers many times, and it does ring true. Life is tough for everyone, Christian and non-Christian. But there is a difference. Life is tough, without meaning and sometimes unbearable for those who do not have a surrendered relationship with God, but it is tough with great meaning and definitely bearable for those who do. Life is not a bowl of cherries, and we cannot pretend differently. Yet with God, it can be a totally victorious life and a joy-filled life. At times the sailing will be smooth, and at other times the storms will howl incessantly. This chapter will discuss a number of those tough times and how real people have handled them.

Once Jesus slept in a small boat during a fierce storm. Perhaps fatigue was a factor, but surrender was the biggest factor. He was so filled with trust in his Father that a storm did not daunt him at all. The longer you live, the more storms you will face. Recently, a friend of mine in his late 30s mentioned that he had lost only one close relative to death, an aged grandmother. That story will change markedly with the passing of a few more years. No one is exempt from the heart-testing, heart-rending trials of life. We may handle the calm times well, but how will we do when the problems multiply and threaten our security to the maximum? Surrender is the only guarantee that no storm of life will swamp your boat.

## Security in the Face of Disrupted Schedules

The challenge of disrupted schedules may appear minor, but at times it can strongly test the level of our surrender. Back in 1981, my wife and I were speaking in New Zealand at an evangelism seminar. It was our first trip out of North America, and we were enthralled with the travel, New Zealand and the seminar.

After a glorious week, the time came for our departure. We went to the small airport in Napier and began check-in procedures. I watched as the gentleman in front of me was routinely checked in for the same flight. However, as soon as I took my place at the counter, the agent took the microphone and announced that the entire transportation system of the country was now officially on strike! My heart started pounding and panic began seeping into my soul. Our children were small and thousands of miles away. What if an emergency arose? What could we do? *Oh, NO!* (Obviously, I knew little about surrender at that point in my life.)

My mind began racing to figure a way out of this dilemma. My first reaction was not to pray; it was to force the issue and find some sort of alternative. I thought about the overseas portion of our flight and realized that it was booked on an American carrier. I rushed to the closest phone and called the carrier at the Auckland airport. They said the 747 was already there for our afternoon flight, and was scheduled to depart on time. I turned to the missionary who had taken us to the airport and asked how far we were from Auckland. "Three hundred and fifty miles," he answered.

"How long to drive that distance?"

"Seven hours, with luck," said he.

Just enough time to make the flight! Amen!

Quickly the arrangements were made and we set off for the big city, driving fast and on the "wrong" side of the road (British system)! The trip took us through some beautiful countryside, but from the passenger side, I was pushing the floorboard with my foot and eating antacid tablets. Seven hours later, we pulled into the parking lot, and I dashed into the airport. Thousands of stranded passengers filled every space. I located the line for my flight and took my place, wondering if any seats would be available by the time those hundreds of other passengers in front of me were checked in. My blood pressure was still elevated and my heartbeat rapid. But I felt much better; not quite relieved, but closer to it. I had almost pulled it off and beat the system. I couldn't wait to see my kids.

Soon my worst fears were realized. The ticket agent announced that although our plane was present, Air New Zealand would not sell them any petrol. *Oh, no! This can't be happening—not to me!* But it was. At that point, I surrendered. Nothing else could be done, and I became completely calm as I finally accepted the inevitable. At that exact moment, I looked out at the dense crowd and my eyes met an Air New Zealand employee's eyes. He looked familiar, and when he shouted "Gordon!" I realized it was Tony from the seminar. He rushed over, asked about our problem and offered a great Plan B. We went to his nearby home and spent a lovely two days being treated as honored guests. Tony and his wife showed us all over the city and poured out that warm Kiwi hospitality.

When the 407 passengers took off two days later, we were on the plane. God took perfectly good care of our children (they were with the grandparents) and provided far more for us than we deserved. But what is the lesson? Just this: I could have been surrendered from the beginning and calmly followed much the same itinerary. If I had started with a trusting prayer, I could have enjoyed the seven hour drive and had my acidic stomach calmed. God was in control all along. I should have been relaxed and rejoicing with that knowledge. I was only being human, you say? It really did no harm after all? Perhaps, but perhaps not. A Bible teacher of mine once said that anxiety is practical atheism. I grimaced when he said it, because in my heart of hearts, I knew he was right. Therefore, during the many hours on that trip to Auckland, I had been atheistic, reacting as if there was no God. Is that so minor after all?

## Security in the Face of Timidity

When I was a young man, my insecurities caused me to be timid, especially in situations which were not under my control. I put up an arrogant, cocky front as a defense mechanism, but it was a thin veneer which often peeled off. One of the biggest barriers to my becoming a spiritual person in my early 20s was the threat of getting honest with myself and others, but I made the decision to do it. Putting that decision into practice was, at times, excruciatingly difficult.

In a young marrieds Bible class, I would often decide to answer a question posed by the teacher and raise my hand to be called on for a response. Once committed to that extent, my heart would start pounding and gradually move up into my throat, causing my tie to jump. At that point, I would lower my hand to save face. During that same period, a certain man would call different men in the church, asking them to lead the various prayers at the services. When he called me, I always informed him that I was unable to do that sort of thing and to please ask someone else. But he kept calling.

One night, he caught me at a weak point, and I said "Yes." After I hung up, I couldn't believe what I had done! All week I was petrified at the thought of standing up in front of 200 people and leading a prayer. Finally, the Sunday night arrived when I was to make my public debut. I prayed that the sermon would last forever. It didn't. Finally, my name was called, and I made my way to the microphone. My knees were knocking and my voice was shaking terribly. Actually, when my first well-rehearsed words came out, it was not my voice—it sounded like a high-pitched woman's voice! I had never felt so embarrassed and humiliated. I was out the door as soon as possible and determined to refuse any public leadership in the future.

A few months later, however, I actually consented to deliver a brief lesson at a midweek service. Scared nearly speechless, I managed to give the lesson without totally embarrassing myself. After I finished, I felt pretty good about myself. About 11 p.m. that night, my wife Theresa began having severe stomach cramps. We eventually went to the emergency room at the hospital, and she ended up being admitted for three days of testing. All of the tests were negative. Several more months passed, and I was asked to address a Bible teachers meeting. I held together for that one reasonably well, but about 11 p.m. that night Theresa began having those cramps again. Back to the hospital for three more days of testing. Nothing abnormal turned up. At that point, we figured out that she was just having sympathetic pains for me. Knowing how petrified my timidity made me, she felt for me and took my pain on herself!

As the months went by, our interest in full-time ministry grew steadily. Through a series of almost unbelievable events, we ended up making a very quick decision on a Monday night to move immediately to another city to attend a school that trained men for the ministry. I left the following Sunday and started school. Theresa stayed behind with our young son to sell the house, and miraculously, it sold in a week. They then joined me in the new city. In the school setting, I felt out of place and totally intimidated. I felt like a lion in a den full of Daniels! I imagined every other person in that school knew more Bible than I did, and probably most of them did.

Since I was a new student and started the new semester a week late, the director of the school wanted me to have a proper introduction. Therefore, he asked me to read a Scripture passage in chapel service at the beginning of my second week. As I walked up to the front of that little chapel, the palpitations erupted. I was terrified again, and as I read the passage, I had to hold the Bible firmly with both hands. I was shaking uncontrollably. Again, the embarrassment and the question, "What am I doing here?"

That night after Theresa and Bryan were asleep upstairs, I went into the kitchen of our apartment and began pouring out my heart to God. "Why did you let me make such a big mistake by moving here? We sold our house, quit our jobs, and sold out for you, and yet I can't even read a scripture. How am I ever going to be able to stand in front of people and preach?" I finally went to bed without an answer. I was confused, frustrated, angry and heartbroken. I felt like a fool and a failure. However, when I awoke the next morning, the answer to my plight was in my mind.

What was the worst thing that could happen to me? I could have a heart attack and die in the pulpit! That was the worst. And I thought to myself, "If I did die trying, surely God will let me into heaven." With that thought to comfort me, I surrendered my timidity and made the firm decision never to refuse an opportunity to serve no matter how strong the fear factor.

Had I imagined at that time what my ministry future would hold, I would never have believed it. The very thought of speaking all over the world to audiences of thousands, writing books and leading groups of all different sizes would have been too much to contemplate. And yet, all of these things have come to pass in spite of the timidity of my basic nature. Knowing myself as I do, I have no doubts that God has done it all. But knowing God as I do, I have no doubts that he would not have done it had I not made the decision to surrender no matter what the cost. The victory of surrender is not theory with me, especially in relation to my timidity; it is quite tangible!

## Security in the Face of Financial Crises

Finances are far too close to many of our hearts. Purse strings and heartstrings are like Siamese twins. As might be expected, God often tests us in this key area, and when we respond to the tests with genuine surrender, his rewards are amazing. I remember a number of times when we decided to contribute money beyond the scope of common sense and put God to the test, so to speak. Actually, Malachi 3:10-11 encourages this kind of testing:

> "Bring the whole tithe into the storehouse, that there may be food in my house. Test me in this," says the LORD Almighty, "and see if I will not throw open the floodgates of heaven and pour out so much blessing that you will not have room enough for it. I will prevent pests from devouring your crops, and the vines in your fields will not cast their fruit," says the LORD Almighty.

When we have made some of these sacrifices, I have seen God keep cars running without breaking down far past a reasonable time and our family remain healthy for abnormally long periods, thus keeping us afloat financially.

One unusual situation I observed in this regard involved a single mother who had made an investment in a friend's business. The friend turned out to be untrustworthy, losing her investment and that of a number of other people. When everything was brought out into the open, it was not a pretty sight. Since all of this took place among friends, a number of emotions came to the surface and were expressed in a meeting of involved parties. Because all were spiritually-minded, more concern about the offender's spiritual well-being was shared than concern for the money lost.

The woman I am describing had invested her life's savings of $9,000. Her comment to the offending person was something to this effect: "I didn't invest anything that I was not willing to lose, but I am very concerned about where you are spiritually and how you are going to respond to your sin." I watched her as she made her comments and thought to myself what a spiritual woman she really was. Genuine concern for the person being addressed was obvious. How many people in her situation would have been so gracious?

Later Satan tempted her to change her heart about her willingness to lose the money. But she remained surrendered and later told of watching God's response. Some years her company gave bonuses and some years they did not. When they were given, the amounts varied considerably, and the most she had ever received was something over $4,000. Not long after she renewed her determination to remain surrendered, she was handed a bonus check. The amount? Take-home pay, after taxes— $9,003! She and I laughed together about God's sense of humor!

## Security in the Face of Family Challenges

Surrender brings some of its greatest tests in our families. Between birth and adulthood, children provide parents with some of life's grandest joys and most significant challenges. Raising children in a world like ours is scary business. The influences for evil are nearly unbelievable, and the opportunities for harm are always present. Parents either wring their hands in anxiety and frustration, or they learn to surrender their children into the hands of God.

When we first moved to Boston seven years ago, our son Bryan was a freshman in college. I knew little about the city and left the details of where he should live in the hands of the campus ministry leaders. He was advised to move in with several other Christian students in an inner-city community. It was very different than the upscale area of San Diego from which Bryan had recently moved. Culture shock set in.

Before long, we all found out that the area where he lived was known to be quite dangerous. The community is in the headlines of the local paper often as drug-related crimes and incidents such as drive-by shootings are reported. Since we were unable to fully support Bryan in school, he needed a good part-time job. The one with the best pay was to work nights as a security guard. The problem was that he did not get off work until just before midnight, and then caught the last subway home. The subway station was a distance from his house, which meant that he walked through a dangerous part of town alone after midnight.

Many nights I was either still up or often woke up, and imagined him walking through those areas at that very moment. The only solution as a parent was to pray and surrender him to God. He never had a serious threat to his life or safety as far as we knew. The experience helped him to deal with things in his character and to grow up. It helped him and his parents to we knew. The experience helped him to deal with things in his character and to grow up. It helped him and his parents to surrender. God was in control, but it took lots of prayer to trust God with Bryan's protection.

Bryan has lived in Honolulu for six years and Renee, our daughter, has lived in cities away from us for the past four, presently in Philadelphia. When they go through struggles, we talk with them long-distance and give all of the input we can. Beyond that, we can't do much except pray. It is an issue of surrender. Even when they were teens at home, we could only do our best and pray about the rest. When either Theresa or I was tempted to be in the panic mode or give up hope in a given situation, one of us had to remind the other that the battle was not yet over. At times, we held on to that thought, prayed, fasted and surrendered. As the years have passed, God has been faithful and has blessed our family. Both of our children are strong disciples of Jesus, and are currently steady dating with very spiritual disciples. We have great relationships with them and their "steadies," and are thankful to God for his answers to thousands of prayers offered with surrendered hearts.

In addition to the prayers of surrender, the element of humility was often the telling factor in making it through the challenging times. Realizing that we were often too close emotionally to the situation, we sought and followed the advice of close friends with spiritual hearts and experiences. Many parents are not open about their family struggles, which blocks them from seeking spiritual counsel. Surrender to God means surrender to the circumstances surrounding our lives and to the people he has placed in them. God, through our family situations, has trained and refined us in many ways. Our part was simply to do all we could with a surrendered spirit before his mighty hand. This faith on our part allowed him to work. How surrendered are you

**Security in the Face of Relationship Challenges**

In the spring of 1985, just before we moved from the state of Washington to San Diego, we were visiting there for the weekend. On Mother's Day, as I remember it, I preached a sermon based on the lost son of Luke 15. After the service, a pretty blond young woman named Cathy asked to talk with me. As she started the conversation, she broke down in tears. The thought that God could still love her and forgive her was overwhelming. I introduced her to a woman who lived in her area who then studied the Bible with her, helping her to become a Christian.

After we moved to the area, she asked if I would come by to meet her reluctant husband and see if he might be persuaded to study the Bible. Jerry was not at all excited about some preacher coming by to visit, but didn't know quite how to refuse without sounding like the bad guy. We ended up hitting it off quite well and became close friends. Within a short time, he was baptized into Christ. The family was now united. Well, sort of.

It turned out that Cathy had been involved in some bitter legal disputes with Andrew, her first husband, concerning their child, who was living with Cathy. As time went by, she determined to put the surrender principle into practice with Andrew and his present wife, Karen. When Karen and Cathy talked to work out visitation times for the shared daughter, Karen noticed a change in Cathy. She asked if it was the new job, to which Cathy replied, "No, it is God." Although it was very difficult, Cathy invited Karen and Andrew to come to a church recreational activity. Amazingly, they came. Then Cathy knew she should invite them to church the following day. She did, and they came.

There was tension in the pew that day. Her husband was on one side of Cathy and her first husband and wife were on the other side. It didn't *feel* right, but she knew it *was* right. Andrew and Karen began studying the Bible and became Christians a short while later. At their baptisms, knowing of the past bitterness and hatred between the two families, I wept as I watched the four embrace one another as brothers and sisters in Christ! Surrender was, for Cathy and Jerry, an extremely difficult proposition in their situation. But they did it, and hearts were cleansed of soul-destroying sins as marvelous healing took place for all to see.

### Security in the Face of Health Threats

Satan's challenge to God regarding Job demonstrates how much a health problem can threaten faith. After killing Job's children and herds, he came back to God with a further challenge to the faith of Job.

> *"Skin for skin!" Satan replied. "A man will give all he has for his own life. But stretch out your hand and strike his flesh and bones, and he will surely curse you to your face" (Job 2:4-5).*

Perhaps nothing reveals the quality of our faith quite like health threats. Thankfully, many devoted disciples have weathered such storms and emerged victorious.

One of my closest friends in Boston is Tom Jones, editor of Discipleship Publications International (DPI). Our backgrounds are very similar in many ways, with both of us having been in the ministry for most of our adult years. Seven years ago, when I first moved to Boston, Tom and I were working closely together. He was struggling with health problems which had not been completely diagnosed, but the likelihood was that he had multiple sclerosis (MS). Being a man of integrity and a tender conscience, he felt bad that he was unable to work in the ministry with the same energy as in past years.

In March of that year, I strongly advised him to leave the ministry position he was in and seek administrative work in the church office. At that point, this seemed the only logical path. However, the decision was heart-rending for him and his family. For several months he worked with financial matters and other

types of office work, fighting both MS, with its attendant fatigue,
and feelings of worthlessness. At that point, he wondered if his
most productive years were over. I could only imagine what a
man in his early 40s was feeling in such a situation and would
have given anything to have relieved his health burdens.

He continued one day at a time to surrender his situation to
God, and seven years later, the providential plan of God has
become much clearer. Romans 8:28 is not simply a nice little
adage to adorn plaques on the wall—it is real life stuff, and Tom's
life and the impact of DPI's publishing ministry provides the
proof. In the preface of his recent book *Mind Change*, he describes
this plan of God in these words:

> You are about to read a sentence that I never thought I
> would write. Here it is: *Multiple sclerosis is one of the best things
> that has ever happened to me.* When I first said that to myself, it
> seemed like a miracle.
>
> I hated the disease. I fought it. I resented it. I looked at
> the people who didn't have it, and I wondered why in the
> world I did. I would think about all the walks I couldn't take,
> all the tennis and golf I couldn't play and the high-energy dad
> I could no longer be. I would wake up in the morning and
> think, "If this is the way life is going to be, I'm not sure I want
> it." I would pray about it but would lose faith even as I prayed.
>
> However, things changed in me, and multiple sclerosis
> (MS) has become one of my most important teachers in God's
> university of life. Sure, I still have some negative feelings about
> it. I struggle when I watch some of you spike a volleyball. I
> long to cast it out when all my energy is gone by the middle of
> the day or when the pain seems unrelenting. I look forward to
> heaven where it will not exist. But I know in my heart of
> hearts that God has used it to change my character and to
> show me something you need to learn just as much as I did:
> *We must be overcomers, and with God's help we can be—whatever
> the challenge.*[1]

[1] Thomas Jones, *Mind Change: The Overcomer's Handbook* (Woburn, Mass.:
Discipleship Publications International, 1994) 10.

Another Boston family showed the power of surrender in the face of an extremely serious health threat. Ron and Jane moved to Boston in the spring of 1989 with hearts full of excitement and dreams. Their plans included getting married, beginning a family and going out on a mission team. A few months later, Jane was diagnosed with ovarian cancer. Major surgery was followed by months of chemotherapy. Ron and Jane faced their uncertain future with the kind of surrender which undoubtedly made the heart of God soar. Ron describes their heart during the early days of this monumental threat to Jane's life:

> There were many decisions to be made during that difficult time. Without a doubt, the easiest was my decision to ask Jane to be my wife. On January 13, 1990, we were married. With faith in God and a commitment to each other, we decided to make the most of whatever time God would give us. More than one argument was resolved by reminding each other that we were wasting valuable time. Honestly, I did not expect to see our first anniversary together.
>
> I could go on and tell you about hospitals, doctors, nurses, surgical procedures, blood tests, alternative cancer treatments—but those things do not tell the real story. The real power and ultimate victory are not found in textbooks or research labs, although I am very thankful we were blessed with some of the best doctors in the world. The real power is found in learning to hold tightly to your relationship with God no matter what the circumstances (Philippians 1:27) and to live a life worthy of the gospel.[2]

In spite of many prayers for Jane to be cured, God's will was that she go home. She passed from this life into glory on November 16, 1993. To watch a young, vivacious woman be ravaged by cancer demands that we be surrendered and seek heaven's perspective. That perspective is described in Psalm

---

[2] Ron Cicerchia, "Finish Strong," *Mind Change: The Overcomer's Handbook* (Woburn, Mass.: Discipleship Publications International) 157.

116:15: "Precious in the sight of the LORD is the death of his saints." The impact of Jane's life was measured in terms of how she handled her illness and impending death. Many people around her during those brief years had their view of God altered in a highly positive way. Only a surrendered, powerful faith could have produced in her the godly responses to pain. Ron concluded his article in *Mind Change* with these thoughts:

> Jane Cicerchia faced all these challenges, and with the power of God, she overcame. She finished the race and finished strong! I will never forget her faith or her love. I consider it an honor and a privilege to have been her husband and friend. The best is yet to be. Hold on tightly. Finish strong![3]

## Security in the Face of Imminent Death

The following account describes one of the most heartbreaking, yet heartwarming, stories I have ever been blessed to experience. Just less than two years ago, one of my favorite people died. When she died, I was asked to write a tribute to have read at her funeral. I have included it here.

*Tribute to Suzanne Atkins*

When the Ferguson family moved to San Diego in June 1985, Suzanne quickly became a part of our family. From the beginning, she discipled [our daughter] Renee, who had just turned 13. In fact, Sue (as we called her back then), was Renee's very first discipler. Then after several months, Theresa started discipling Sue. She fit very well with the Ferguson women—short, cute and *full of spunk*! To put it another way, they were all real *characters* together. My relationship with Suzanne was very special. In the kingdom, I have many daughters. But there are a select few who are totally like daughters in the flesh, as far as the heart ties go. Suzanne was a part of that select few to me. The bond between

[3] Cicerchia, p. 159.

us was in some ways better felt than told, though we were both expressive about the love we had for one another. Our family shared many wonderful moments together with Suzanne, and the impact she had on all of us will not be fully understood and appreciated until all of us are in heaven.

I remember when she and Dave started going steady. She was so excited that her face was locked in a permanent grin. She had a wonderful way of being excited just like a little child, infecting everyone around with her joy. That part of her remained until the very end. Those of us who came to see her in the hospital came for the purpose of encouraging her, but it totally went the opposite direction—she encouraged everyone who came in an absolutely *amazing* way! But, back to her relationship with Dave. After they had gone steady for what seemed a *long* time, Suzanne was getting a little desperate for a marriage proposal. Therefore, I stepped in as old *Dad*. Dave and I went out for some time together one day, and I finally got to the point of the visit as I asked him, "Son, just what are your intentions toward my daughter?"

He explained that he loved her and wanted to marry her, but he was far too vague about the timing to suit me (and to suit Suzanne for sure!). I gave him the challenge to either propose or to break up with Suzanne in order for her to find someone really serious about marriage. Dave's face turned pale, and he began to make far more urgent plans. Within a short time, they were engaged, and before long, Theresa, Renee and I were a part of a great wedding! To state that it was a happy occasion would be putting it mildly. In the years since, we have been so proud of Dave and Suzanne and the wonderful little family with which God has blessed them.

The brevity of time that Suzanne was given to live, to love and to have a family was far too short from our human point of view. On the other hand, millions of unhappy people would gladly trade their many years of disillusionment and frustration for her brief years of true joy. When you consider her salvation as a part of the picture, her life was a glorious one indeed. The *quality* of life is far more important than the *quantity* of life. Suzanne grabbed life by the throat and experienced what Jesus called the *abundant life*.

I do not feel sorry for her in any way whatsoever. She lived her life, made her mark on eternity, and left with radiant joy. I will *never ever* forget the way she faced death. Having heard about her amazing attitudes, I came to visit her a few days before she died already tremendously encouraged. My first words to her were something like this: "Hey, kid—what in the world are you still doing here anyway?" Her reply was something like this: "Well, I didn't want to be, but I guess that God wanted me to see old Dad one more time [referring to me]." Truthfully, old Dad needed to see how she viewed death in order to be much better prepared to face his own end.

After a prayer of victory, I shared my favorite passage of Scripture with her, 2 Corinthians 4:16-18, which reads:

> *Therefore we do not lose heart. Though outwardly we are wasting away, yet inwardly we are being renewed day by day. For our light and momentary troubles are achieving for us an eternal glory that far outweighs them all. So we fix our eyes not on what is seen, but on what is unseen. For what is seen is temporary, but what is unseen is eternal.*

As I left that hospital room with a lump in my throat and tears in my eyes, her last words were, "I'll see you on the other side." She was like a kid lined up at the merry-go-round waiting her turn. She was so excited to go, and without question, so *prepared* to go. I miss her, and my heart is hurting, but I envy her spirit, her completely spiritual view of death, and now the reward that she is already enjoying. Hundreds of lives will never be the same without her, but praise God, hundreds of lives will never be the same *because* of her. My life is one of those, and I now await the time when I can share all of these deep emotions with her face-to-face in the very presence of God himself. Lord, speed the day!

## Theresa's Tribute

My wife also wrote a very moving account of her final time with Suzanne just before she died. The following is an excerpt from her tribute:

> You glorified God by totally surrendering to God's will and at the same time influenced as many people as possible to trust God as well. Your total surrender of Dave and the boys to God without anger, doubt or self-pity was a powerful tribute to your faith. You said: "Dave will remain faithful!" I know God accomplished his plan for you in the 32 years that he gave you to live. As Acts 13:36 says of David: "For when David had served God's purpose in his own generation, he fell asleep." You fell asleep but awakened with eternal life with God! Since it is your physical birthday on Monday, August 23rd, you just had an early birthday celebration with God and many, many others!
>
> My most impactful memory of you was the night of August 11, 1993. I was with you in the hospital, and you asked me with a sparkle in your eyes, "Theresa, how would you feel if you were going to die right now?" I said, "I'd be so happy to at last see God and Jesus." I asked you, "How do you feel about dying?" Your face lit up with a radiant smile and a sparkle in your eyes that I'll never ever forget. You said one word—"EXCITED!" The joy that I saw! The radiance that I saw! The sparkle in your eyes that I saw! A burst of excitement ran through me from my head to my toes. I felt a burst of excitement from you, for you had come to the finish line in your race and were about to finish and meet God and Jesus there! Your confidence, peace, joy and total surrender will never be forgotten, and I plan to follow your example.

*Postscript*

Dave faced Suzanne's death with the same surrendered heart she had. After her death, he dealt with the loss and pain in a deeply spiritual way. Because he has two young children, Dave was encouraged to begin dating fairly soon. Even though it was difficult at first, he started taking out sisters who had similar needs. Soon, he met a woman who had been a single mom for several years before becoming a Christian. They both found the attraction growing, and in time, began dating steadily. Dave called us to let us know that God was kind and taking care of him. Some months ago when we were out of town, we returned home to find a message on our answering machine announcing their engagement.

While preparing this chapter, I called his number in San Diego and a woman answered. When I asked for Dave, she told me that he had already gone to work. After stammering around a little, I asked who she was. "Dave's wife, Mary," she replied. We talked for awhile and became acquainted over the phone. She was so warm, friendly and spiritually minded that I hung up the phone with a heart bursting with joy and gratitude. Suzanne is in heaven smiling as she watches Mary love her husband and children. All is well, for the God of all comfort has never let spiritual surrender go unrewarded. Casting ourselves on God is the only logical path to the door of death and beyond into the eternity behind it. When we can look death in the face, and yet remain totally secure and full of hope, surrender has met its finest hour!

PART

# Surrender: The Biblical Principles

# CHAPTER 5

# Finding Life Through Death

Then he called the crowd to him along with his disciples and said: "If anyone would come after me, he must deny himself and take up his cross and follow me. For whoever wants to save his life will lose it, but whoever loses his life for me and for the gospel will save it. What good is it for a man to gain the whole world, yet forfeit his soul? Or what can a man give in exchange for his soul? If anyone is ashamed of me and my words in this adulterous and sinful generation, the Son of Man will be ashamed of him when he comes in his Father's glory with the holy angels (Mark 8:34-38).*

The setting of these words has everything to do with their meaning and application. In the preceding verses, Jesus foretold his impending death in no uncertain terms. Peter, in his usual blunt way, took exception to the prophecy of Jesus. In fact, he went so far as to rebuke Jesus. In reply, Jesus distinguished the difference between humanism and righteousness:

> But when Jesus turned and looked at his disciples, he rebuked Peter. "Get behind me, Satan!" he said. "You do not have in mind the things of God, but the things of men" (Mark 8:33).

The things of men are tantamount to self-preservation, while the things of God are equated with complete self-denial. Hence, he talks of dying to self, losing our life.

## The Scope of Jesus' Demands: Everyone

Peter's actions seem to us fairly extreme, and yet our reactions to self-denial are not very different. We are not only protective of ourselves, but we are protective of those closest to us. We would love to be able to believe that the price of following Jesus is not as radical as he states. Have you never wished that it would be enough to be reasonably good morally, attend a nice little neighborhood church regularly, and then be able to focus on self-interests the rest of the week? I was raised believing that exact philosophy.

As I grew up, I was not particularly searching for spiritual meaning to life or for any kind of personal relationship with God. But I did go to church every week—my mother made sure of that! Although I was not overly interested in spiritual matters, I did feel better when I went to church. I saw religion as something like a fire insurance policy. I was looking for maximum benefits for the cheapest premium, but I definitely didn't want to face the fire without it! In other words, I wanted enough religion to insure myself against hell, but I didn't want to get carried away with it and become a fanatic. To be honest, it never occurred to me that this approach was so far off. It is the philosophy of the large majority of religious people in America.

However, the philosophy of heaven is quite different! Jesus does not beat around the bush in describing the only kind of religion acceptable to him and the Father. He starts off in Mark 8:34 describing the scope of his demands: *Anyone* who would come after him must deny himself. This passage and the Great Commission in Matthew 28:18-20 show that God expects no less commitment from the "average" member as from the apostles themselves. The clergy/laity double standard is a doctrine of demons and a tool of the devil.

Years ago, I was invited to meet with some church leaders about the possibility of my moving to serve as their evangelist. About ten minutes into the conversation, the lead elder (by influence, not title) said something along these lines: "Well, Gordon, we have many young people who can fly with the eagles, and we want them to be challenged to do that. On the other hand, we have many older members who aren't eagles, and they shouldn't be made to feel inferior or guilty about that." Of course, I totally agreed that all disciples have different gifts and abilities and are at different places in both understanding of spiritual matters and in spiritual maturity. However, that elder was discussing differing *commitment levels*, which was another matter entirely. All who follow Jesus must be sold out to serving him and advancing his cause on the earth. Our performance will vary incredibly, for the reasons stated above, but our commitment cannot. (No, I did not accept the position with that church. Even in those days I knew better than to try to work with that kind of leadership!)

## The Price of Jesus' Demands: Death

Death to self is described in the following ways in Mark 8: Deny self; take up your cross, and lose your life for Jesus and the gospel. But just what does "death to self" mean in a practical sense? For one thing, it means that we are not seeking self-satisfaction and personal gratification. Rather, we are seeking to please God on an all-day, every-day basis. We are to follow Jesus, and here is how he described his goal in life: "For I seek not to please myself but him who sent me" (John 5:30), and "The one who sent me is with me; he has not left me alone, for I always do what pleases him" (John 8:29). Therefore, every decision in our lives must be made with these two questions in mind: "What would Jesus do in this situation?" and "What would please God?"

Dealing with our emotions is essential if we are to meet Jesus' demands. Most of our decisions are based on emotions, no matter how we attempt to rationalize to the contrary. I once read about an experiment conducted with engineers to determine the basis of their decisions. Of course, we would assume that those who used their intellectual faculties all day long in their profession would be intellectually focused in all decision-making. Such was not the case. They may have been more proficient than some in justifying their decisions intellectually, but like all other humans, the most important factor influencing their decisions was emotion. We do most of what we do because of how we *feel* about doing it.

How can we avoid being ruled by emotional self-interest? By imitating Jesus. In the Garden of Gethsemane, he poured out his heart to God and expressed all of his feelings. He did not *want* to go to the cross. Self cried out for deliverance! Yet, he always concluded his prayers with "Not my will but your will be done." We all have feelings, opinions and preferences. God is quite willing for us to share all of these things with him. On the other hand, he is quite unwilling for that to be the end of the matter. We must be open to accepting the *opposite* of what we feel, if doing so is his will.

How do you know whether or not something is God's will? Study of the biblical principles which relate to the decision is a must. Praying for insight is another must. However, another must involves seeking advice from spiritual people. Without that input, we can easily be fooled about how much our own emotions are controlling us. As the writer of Proverbs put it, "The way of a fool seems right to him, but a wise man listens to advice" (Proverbs 12:15), and further, "There is a way that seems right to a man, but in the end it leads to death" (Proverbs 14:12). (For more discussion on finding God's will, see the Appendix on p. 211.)

Without godly input from another person, we are caught up in a "closed" system of reasoning. We may be looking at something about our lives in a skewed way and not realize it. Within a closed system of reasoning, $2 + 2 = 6$ can seem unquestionably true every time you add up the components of the equation. But the Proverbs writer has something to say on this point also: "The first to present his case seems right, till another comes forward and questions him" (Proverbs 18:17). The proverb is *especially* true when *you* are that first person. Since the decision about *your* life affects *you* most, you are often the least capable of making an unbiased decision. Without input, you will likely be ruled by emotions without even realizing it.

The pop song "You Light Up My Life" expresses such erroneous reasoning in this manner: "It can't be wrong when it feels so right." If all the mistakes made following this philosophy just in the sphere of romance were written down, the pages would reach from here to the moon and back! It *can* be wrong when it feels so right. It often *is* wrong when it feels so right. "If it feels good, then do it," we reason. "Whatever *seems* right to you must *be* right for you," say our feelings. Nothing could be further from the truth and from the cross of Jesus Christ! God's will for us is often very different from what feels good at the moment. What if Jesus had done in the garden what felt best to him? You and I and everyone else would be bound for hell!

Once, I was trying to make some major decisions about my life, and sharing my thinking with a mature brother. I thought my reasoning process was nearly infallible, since it seemed so logical and reasonable to me. He kept disagreeing with me, but I wouldn't let him break into my closed system of reasoning. Eventually I left without being persuaded in the least by him. On the way home, I came to my senses and realized how foolish I had been. As soon as I arrived at my house, I called back to apologize and assured him that I would accept his unbiased advice. Looking back now, I can see how disastrous my decision would have been to me and to everyone I hold dear. Praise God that I did not ultimately subscribe to the "It can't be wrong when it feels so right" philosophy!

I remember trying to break into the closed thinking system of a dear friend some years back. He had come to conclusions with which all of his coworkers in the ministry strongly disagreed. some lengthy and intense discussions with him, he concluded with something like this: "Well, Gordon, thank you for the time and input. Now I will pray about it, and then do what seems best to me." That reply sounds rather noble and seems quite normal, doesn't it? It is anything but noble, although it is normal and common to man.

Trying to disguise our selfish decisions with spiritual-sounding terminology may fool us, and even others, temporarily, but it never fools God and never works best in the long run. Yet, such terminology abounds: "The Lord led me to..." "I felt the prompting of the Holy Spirit..." "God spoke to my spirit and said..." Such pious cover-ups for self-willed decisions remind me of two "preacher" stories.

A younger preacher was bragging about his lack of sermon preparation by claiming that the Lord spoke to him directly when he stood up to preach, thus providing his sermon. An older preacher commented that the Lord had only spoken to him once in that regard. The younger man asked what God had said to him on that one occasion, to which the older man replied: "God said to me, 'Smith, you're *lazy!*'"

Another preacher came home one afternoon and informed his wife that he had been offered another preaching job in a nearby town which paid $500 a month more than his present position. He said to her, "Honey, we need to seek God's will in this matter. Why don't I go upstairs and pray about it, while you stay downstairs and start packing up the kitchen?"

As an older man, most of my decisions are now based on the spiritual advice of mature people. I do not accept such advice without doing my own thinking, studying and praying, but I have learned to trust other reliable spiritual leaders more than myself in cases where my self-interests are at stake. The closer you are emotionally to a decision, the less likely you are to independently make the right decision. Some of the most difficult decisions I have made in the past decade, which have had the greatest impact on me and my family, have been made in direct opposition to my emotions in the matter. Yet, I now look at the results of those decisions and thank God that he taught me enough about surrender to keep me from being ruled by self.

Some of you are reading this and feeling either fear or a bit of indignation. The idea of trusting the advice of others instead of your own feelings in making key decisions may seem ludicrous. But have we not already proved how opposite the cross is to humanism? Did we not admit how paradoxical the ways of God are? Where is the cross in this business called "surrender" if not in denial of self and of our own feelings? Which parent ever *felt like* changing a dirty diaper, or *felt like* getting up in the middle of the night to attend to a child who had vomited all over himself and his bed? Righteousness nearly always goes against the grain initially, and selfishness always goes with the flow of our humanness. We either deny self and take up a cross daily, or we are none of his. Surrender cannot be compromised.

## The Focus of Jesus' Demands: Spiritual Purpose

In this account in Mark 8, Jesus clearly describes the focus of the Christian's life. We are to follow him as our example and model. John put it this way in 1 John 2:6: "Whoever claims to live in him must walk as Jesus did." Therefore, since he lost his life in the accomplishment of his mission, it is logical to expect that we are to lose our lives for him and the gospel. But what does it mean to lose our lives for him and his message?

We gain some insight into the answer by realizing most of the apostles literally lost their physical lives for the gospel, as did thousands of disciples in the early centuries of the church. They had a focus which prompted this shocking reaction by those not following Jesus. What caused them to lose their lives? It was not simply living by Jesus' moral teaching. The world may not like our standards, but it usually will not kill us or persecute us for living by them. The opposition comes when we forcefully share the gospel! When we take up the mission of Jesus to spread his teaching all over the world, then we are following in his steps and can expect similar treatment to that received by him. Make no mistake about it, surrender to Jesus is surrender to his mission. And this kind of purpose in our lives will guarantee a backlash. Consider Jesus' words in John 15:18-20:

> *"If the world hates you, keep in mind that it hated me first. If you belonged to the world, it would love you as its own. As it is, you do not belong to the world, but I have chosen you out of the world. That is why the world hates you. Remember the words I spoke to you: 'No servant is greater than his master.' If they persecuted me, they will persecute you also. If they obeyed my teaching, they will obey yours also."*

Jesus further explains our purpose in Mark 8 as one that is opposite the purpose of gaining the whole world. Speaking of material things, Jesus said: "For the pagans run after all these things, and your heavenly Father knows that you need them" (Matthew 6:32). Life does not consist in the abundance of possessions (Luke 12:15), the American Dream notwithstanding! When we pursue these things, we get our spirituality choked out by the worries of life and the deceitfulness of wealth (Mark 4:19).

A focus on the physical aspects of life makes us much more prone to be ashamed of Jesus and his words. Standing up for righteousness in an increasingly pagan society cannot be done unless we are truly seeking Jesus and his kingdom as our first priority in life. Surrender to the purposes of Jesus on the earth will give us the convictions and courage to shout the word of the gospel from the rooftops. In the context of evangelizing, Jesus said

> *"Whoever acknowledges me before men, I will also acknowledge him before my Father in heaven. But whoever disowns me*

*before men, I will disown him before my Father in heaven"*
*(Matthew 10:32-33).*

The emotion which we must deny over and over is that of
*fear*, and this emotion is more pervasive when we are sharing our
faith than at any other time.

Surrender, or death to self, is never simply a good suggestion
that we can take or leave. It is part and parcel of following Jesus.
No accountable person fulfills his purpose on earth or enters
heaven without surrendering to the mission and purposes of
Jesus. None of us ever does this perfectly, but the intentions of
our hearts must be unmistakably aimed at this goal. When we
are motivated by the cross of Jesus Christ to surrender our will
to God's will, we die in order to live, and we live in order to die.

CHAPTER 6

# A Daily Cross Equals Discipleship

The book of Luke was written by a Gentile to a Gentile audience. A major emphasis of the book is on *repentance*, since the lifestyle of disciples was radically different from that of pagans in first-century society. Interestingly, in Luke's account of the Great Commission (Luke 24:44-49), he mentions neither faith nor baptism specifically (although both are included in the plan as we know from other texts). Rather, he simply mentions repentance since that aspect of accepting Jesus was their greatest challenge. It should be rather obvious that our "Gentile" society has much the same challenge to face in accepting Jesus as Lord of their lives.

## Daily Cross Bearing

Repentance in Luke means what it does in the other gospels—living as a disciple. As we saw in Mark 8, it means taking up the cross. However, Luke records one additional clarifying word in Luke 9:23-26: "take up your cross *daily*" (emphasis added). This business of surrender is not something we take care of for all time at baptism. Just when we think we have everything in place, changing circumstances can bring up new areas in which we must surrender. Unless there is a decision that we will deny self and go to the cross day after day after day as long as it takes, we will be relying on a humanistic escape plan and are bound to fail.

In Luke 9:57-62, Jesus provides some practical applications of what daily cross-bearing involves.

> As they were walking along the road, a man said to him, "I will follow you wherever you go." Jesus replied, "Foxes have holes and birds of the air have nests, but the Son of Man has no place to lay his head."
>
> He said to another man, "Follow me." But the man replied, "Lord, first let me go and bury my father."
>
> Jesus said to him, "Let the dead bury their own dead, but you go and proclaim the kingdom of God."
>
> Still another said, "I will follow you, Lord; but first let me go back and say good-by to my family."
>
> Jesus replied, "No one who puts his hand to the plow and looks back is fit for service in the kingdom of God."

The first man pledged his allegiance to Jesus and then had that allegiance tested quickly by Jesus, who requires anyone who would follow him to count the cost. A choice with such far-reaching consequences to a person's life cannot be made without knowing and thinking through the demands involved. Therefore, Jesus checked out his materialism. No man can serve two masters, and our desire for money and possessions can certainly master our hearts and lives.

The second man was asked by Jesus to follow him, and he quickly made a family excuse. Many in his culture viewed the personal care of aged parents as an obligation for the lifetime of the parent. Likely, Jesus was not forbidding the man to bury his father in the literal sense of merely arranging his funeral. Rather, he was telling the man that even an important obligation like the one to care for family must become secondary to the kingdom of God. (A hard teaching!) The man's real problem, however, was not found in wanting to care for his father, but in telling Jesus "First let me..." (He could have used Jabay's book *The God Players!*) Discipleship involves saying "First you, Lord," not "First me."

Similarly, the third man had a family excuse, but more importantly, he also had the "First let me..." attitude. Both men had to understand that discipleship is not an offer we make to

Jesus on our terms, however good they sound to us. Had these men unconditionally surrendered to Jesus' lordship, it is possible he would have then told them to go deal with their family obligations. But until they were surrendered to him, even a well-meant action would not have had a good result.

In this passage Jesus demonstrates the impossibility of making radical kingdom decisions while holding on to the physical world. Material possessions are not wrong in and of themselves, but they can easily possess us. Family responsibilities are real, and must be factored into our lives—yet nothing tests our hearts quite like family. Jesus forces us to deal with the potential problems *before* making the ultimate decision to follow him. Luke 14 will make this principle clear, as we will see later.

Making the decision to follow Jesus, to be his disciple, is no light matter. Listen to these words from Matthew 10:34-37:

> *"Do not suppose that I have come to bring peace to the earth. I did not come to bring peace, but a sword. For I have come to turn*
>
> > *'a man against his father,*
> > *a daughter against her mother,*
> > *a daughter-in-law against her mother-in-law—*
> > *a man's enemies will be the members*
> > *of his own household.'*
>
> *Anyone who loves his father or mother more than me is not worthy of me; anyone who loves his son or daughter more than me is not worthy of me..."*

Taking up a cross daily means that Jesus' will is more important to us than the comforts of life or the presence of family. Further, it means that following him is more important than the *approval* of family. This issue may be our biggest challenge. Forfeiting approval from our dearest relationships is surrender indeed.

As everything in this chapter shows, following Jesus is radical business. It means committing ourselves to a radical lifestyle, undertaking a radical mission and being intimately connected to a group that will certainly appear radical to the world. Often it will be family members who will object most strongly to our involvement in the practice of basic discipleship. Nothing may test our willingness to surrender more. Will we do the will of God even when loved ones are accusing us of foolishness? Will we stand firmly with Jesus Christ even when others are attacking our love, our loyalty and our common sense?

## The Cost of Discipleship

One of the strongest passages in the gospel accounts is Luke 14:25-33.

> [25]Large crowds were traveling with Jesus, and turning to them he said: [26]"If anyone comes to me and does not hate his father and mother, his wife and children, his brothers and sisters—yes, even his own life—he cannot be my disciple. [27]And anyone who does not carry his cross and follow me cannot be my disciple.
>
> [28]"Suppose one of you wants to build a tower. Will he not first sit down and estimate the cost to see if he has enough money to complete it? [29]For if he lays the foundation and is not able to finish it, everyone who sees it will ridicule him, [30]saying, 'This fellow began to build and was not able to finish.'
>
> [31]"Or suppose a king is about to go to war against another king. Will he not first sit down and consider whether he is able with ten thousand men to oppose the one coming against him with twenty thousand? [32]If he is not able, he will send a delegation while the other is still a long way off and will ask for terms of peace. [33]In the same way, any of you who does not give up everything he has cannot be my disciple."

Isn't Jesus amazing? When religious leaders today manage to attract a crowd, they do all they can to keep them around. Jesus seemed to be *trying* to run them off! Three times in this passage, he said "unless" you meet a difficult challenge, you "cannot be my disciple." These three things go a long way in defining discipleship and its inherent surrender.

### "Hate" Your Family

First, in verse 26, he says that we must "hate" our family. Many people, when reading this for the first time, blurt out "That's not right!" It does seem wrong to our ears, doesn't it? However, it is one of the costs of discipleship. We often quickly explain that it means to "love less." While the explanation is not untrue (when compared with Matthew 10:37), we may be lessening the impact of Jesus' words unnecessarily. If he had wanted to say merely "love less," he could have done it. Using the normal Greek word for "hate" throughout this passage, he perhaps gives us the key to understanding his meaning when he says that a disciple must "hate even his own life." He obviously is not talking about our normal way of hating (nor could he be, considering his teaching about showing love, even to enemies). At the very least, he is saying that our relationship with him is to be far more important to us than any human relationship. While the thought of giving up close relationships is threatening, it has often been demanded of Jesus' followers. But beyond that, he is saying that we must "hate" the whole priority system we have set up that puts our human relationships and especially our own feelings and desires above our relationship to God. To become a disciple we must radically reprioritize. The result will be a heart to really love people in the right way with the right motives.

### Carry Your Cross: Persecution

Second, in verse 27, he says that we must take up our cross or we cannot be his disciple. In the first century, a cross was an instrument of ultimate persecution and death. Today, people speak of "bearing their cross" when contemplating the normal challenges of life, such as health problems, relationship difficulties, or financial hardships. As challenging as these things might be, they are not what Jesus had in mind. Bearing a cross involves facing the struggles which come our way *because we are following him*, not the everyday struggles we face because we are human. Persecution is one of the most obvious applications of this cross-bearing.

In 2 Timothy 3:12, Paul writes: "In fact, everyone who wants to live a godly life in Christ Jesus will be persecuted." The presence of persecution does not prove that an individual or spiritual group is godly. It is possible to be persecuted for the wrong things. On the other hand, the *absence* of persecution says much about the lack of true outspoken godliness! Are you willing to stand up and stand out for Jesus—to be called names and be derided for what you believe? If not, you are neither godly nor surrendered. And although you can be religious and a member of a religious group, you cannot be a disciple of Jesus in this unsurrendered condition.

## Give Up Your Possessions

The third "cannot" in Luke 14 is in verse 33. Unless we give up everything we have, we cannot be his disciple. The New American Standard Bible (NASB) translates it "give up all his own possessions." Since our heartstrings are closely connected to our purse strings, this is a real cost to count. What does Jesus mean? He definitely taught that his followers should give financially to the work of the kingdom, to "lay up treasures in heaven." But he meant far more than this in Luke 14.

The real issue here is one of ownership. As disciples of Jesus, we are no longer owners. Rather, we are now managers of the possessions we have turned over to Jesus. Sharecroppers are those who live on another's land, work his fields, live in his house, and drive his vehicles. In turn, food, clothing and shelter are provided by the owner. Similarly, we are managers of God's possessions. They are no longer ours. In fact, absolutely nothing belongs to us, including our families and our own lives. The early church understood the principle well, having seen it lived out in the lives of Jesus and his apostles. Luke records in the book of Acts, "All the believers were together and had everything in common. Selling their possessions and goods, they gave to anyone as he had need" (Acts 2:44-45), and "All the believers were one in heart and mind. No one claimed that any of his possessions was his own, but they shared everything they had" (Acts 4:32).

*Counting the Cost*

In Luke 14:28-32, two powerful illustrations of cost-counting are given. Jesus did not want followers who would leave when the challenges of discipleship mounted. Someone once said that the reason more are not Christians is because they have either seen a Christian or they have not. In other words, they have seen a hypocrite and been turned off to the real thing, or they have never seen a true Christian and been drawn to Jesus as a result. In Revelation 3:15-16, Jesus said that being "cold" spiritually was preferable to being "lukewarm." The cold person makes no profession to be a Christian, while the lukewarm person does. But in their lukewarmness (hypocrisy), they turn the stomachs— and the hearts—of potential believers.

The need to count the cost is clear from this passage, but what is the exact nature of that cost? The passage itself shows that it includes the "hating" of family, the bearing of a cross, and the giving up of all possessions. Without a doubt, the cost is high! Years ago, I began to study Luke 14 in earnest. The more I understood it, the more conviction I felt. As a minister, I was aware of my limited commitment, but I felt better when comparing myself to many members of the churches in which I served. I reasoned something like this: "I may only be 80% committed (I was generous with that figure!), but most of the members are probably only 50% committed."

However, as I studied Luke 14 in conjunction with the account of the rich young ruler, I came to some sobering realizations. That ruler had many positive attributes. He was characterized by following the morals of the Law and no doubt gave at least a tithe of his money. Since he was rich, his tithe was a large amount. (He would be more than welcome in many churches today!) But while he gave *much*, he did not give up *everything* as he was challenged to do by Jesus. In essence, he drew a line and said, "This much and no more." Similarly, I had drawn some lines in my life as well. By comparing myself with others, I had missed the whole point. Jesus was as concerned with my 20% lack of commitment as with someone else's 50% lack. In either case, we had drawn lines and said, "No more."

Giving up everything means more than giving up possessions, to be sure. It means time, reputation, selfishness and many other things. But it does include possessions. During my earliest study of Luke 14, as mentioned above, my conscience began to nag me about one specific possession. I had a very nice fishing boat equipped with many accessories. In fact, I spent more time installing gadgets than actually using the boat for fishing. That boat was my pride and joy. Truthfully, it had become an idol, for in my heart, it was *my* boat, not God's.

My conscience began to bother me when I applied Luke 14:33 to my boat, but one night my wife brought my priority problem to a head. I had been working for hours installing a new gadget. After finishing, I sat in one of the captain's chairs drinking a cup of coffee and admiring my work. Theresa came out in the garage where I kept the boat, saw me sitting in it, and asked me, "Well, Gordon, are you going to kiss it goodnight?" I flushed with anger, but in my heart, I knew she had hit a real nerve! Shortly afterwards, I put an ad in the paper. One woman called for information and commented that my price was high for the age of the boat. I told her about all of the improvements, assuring her that the first to see it would buy it. A short time later, she and her husband came to see it. As I showed them the different features, she turned to me and actually said this: "Mister, if we buy your boat, will you cry?" I almost fainted with shock! I must have been a bigger idolater than I had ever realized. I told her, "Probably, but it's a great boat and you ought to buy it." They did (and no, I didn't actually cry!).

At about that time, I came up with a little formula for dealing with priority problems of whatever type. The formula was *evaluate, regulate* or *amputate*. Priorities must undergo evaluation. If they are getting off-center, the time to regulate comes to help us keep them on track. If regulation does not alleviate the problem, then we must amputate. Jesus did say,

> "If your hand or your foot causes you to sin cut it off and throw it away. It is better for you to enter life maimed or crippled than to have two hands or two feet and be thrown into eternal fire" (Matthew 18:8).

Years later, I did own another boat for a while. My tendency toward idolatry pushed me to the "regulate" stage, but I did not have to amputate it!

**Enjoying the Dividends**

While the costs of discipleship are high (complete surrender), the benefits are far higher. No matter what we give or give up, we can never outgive the most generous Giver of all. The giving side of following Jesus may look high, but it is nothing in comparison to the receiving side. Life comes through death, and freedom through slavery. Ceasing to be a *possessor* means that we also cease to be *possessed*.

Back in 1981, I ordered a new car before we were scheduled to move to the West Coast from Texas. It was only a little Ford

Escort station wagon, but we were excited about it. Finally, after several months, it arrived—complete with luggage rack, tape deck, cruise control and fire-engine red paint! On our moving trip, we had our surrender tested. Just before we entered the town in Oregon where we had motel reservations, a deer appeared out of nowhere on the interstate highway. Given his speed and ours, a collision could not be avoided. Fortunately, he was running so fast that he had almost reached the side of the road before we hit him. Although we had no major wreck, the right front fender of the car was damaged substantially. (Yes, animal lovers, the deer survived.)

We had a choice about how to react to the damage to our new car. One, we could have said, "Oh no! That stupid deer messed up our new car, and it's only the second new one we have ever owned. We just can't believe it. How terrible!" Two, if we were truly surrendered and in line with Luke 14:33, we could have said, "Lord, wow! Did you see that deer run into your car? I guess you did, since it's your car and your deer. Thanks for protecting us. Now we will try to take care of your car and get it fixed." Thankfully, we did react much like the latter example. The story sounds humorous, but it illustrates the point well. If it all belongs to God anyway, nothing is left to worry about. If it's his, let him do the worrying! He promised to do it (Luke 12:29-31); why not let him?

Within a few months after the deer incident, we had purchased the house I mentioned in Chapter One. After another few months, the remodeling had made it much more attractive and livable. Then my surrender got tested by a five-year-old hyperactive boy. He accompanied his mother when she came over to visit Theresa. That afternoon when I arrived home, Theresa informed me about the damage caused by the little guy. He had jerked on the chain pull for the ceiling fan/lamp combination, breaking it off up in the housing where it could not be reached.

Again I had choices. Either moan and bemoan my bad luck, hoping that the kid would never again come to my house or tell God what he already knew—that his fan had been broken by one of his creatures! I remained calm, called my remodeling expert buddy, and prepared to repair God's fan. When Ed came over and tore into the electrical housing of the fan, he asked me who had installed the fan originally. I told him Fred and I had. He then told me we had installed it incorrectly and were lucky it had not caught on fire and burned the whole house down. *Amazing!* That rambunctious little lad might as well have been an angel in disguise! He may have saved our lives as well as our house.

Being uptight and unsurrendered is a poor choice when God has promised to work out all things for our good (Romans 8:28). The cost of discipleship is unconditional surrender, but the dividends are joy and peace. Why worry about what does not belong to you anyway? Why not relax and enjoy the scenery in this magnificent world which God has loaned you? Quit worrying about the price of surrender and revel in its rewards. God is the perfect provider who wants to protect you from all that harms and give you all that blesses. When you do count the cost and surrender, feel blessed, not deprived!

CHAPTER 7

# Dying to Bear Fruit

**N**ow there were some Greeks among those who went up to worship at the Feast. <sup>21</sup>They came to Philip, who was from Bethsaida in Galilee, with a request. "Sir," they said, "we would like to see Jesus." <sup>22</sup> Philip went to tell Andrew; Andrew and Philip in turn told Jesus.

<sup>23</sup>Jesus replied, "The hour has come for the Son of Man to be glorified. <sup>24</sup> I tell you the truth, unless a kernel of wheat falls to the ground and dies, it remains only a single seed. But if it dies, it produces many seeds. <sup>25</sup>The man who loves his life will lose it, while the man who hates his life in this world will keep it for eternal life. <sup>26</sup>Whoever serves me must follow me; and where I am, my servant also will be. My Father will honor the one who serves me" (John 12:20-26).

Only through God could death bring glorification. He rejoices in bringing life from death, be it in more ordinary ways such as ushering in the springtime, or in extraordinary ways as in raising Jesus from the dead. The coming of the Greeks[1] to see Jesus reminded him of his approaching death for all men, including the Gentiles. He then used an agricultural analogy to demonstrate the necessity of his impending death, followed by an immediate application to men. If we love our lives (the physical, worldly aspects), we lose them; if we hate the self-focused life with its wrong priorities, we keep spiritual life for eternity. Those who follow him by dying to self are honored by the Father.

Death brings life. Examples from nature abound. For instance, the female salmon swims upstream, lays

---

[1] Possibly Grecian Jews like those in Acts 6, Greek converts to Judaism or God-fearing Greeks like those in Acts 17:4.

her eggs and dies. Many mothers in the animal world give their lives in protecting their young. Countless human mothers through the centuries have died in giving birth. In the case of plants, the seed must die in order to reproduce, just as Jesus said in the text. All fruitfulness relates to the death/life principle in one way or another. Bearing fruit spiritually is no exception.

Jesus said in John 12:32, "But I, when I am lifted up from the earth, will draw all men to myself." In his three year ministry, he attracted the attention of thousands, many of whom joined the crowds who followed him. Their eyes were opened wide with amazement as they saw him heal the sick and crippled, feed the hungry, restore sight to the blind, and raise the dead. Some saw him walk on the water and instantaneously calm storms with but a few words. He taught in a way which caused even those sent to arrest him to say, "No one ever spoke the way this man does" (John 7:46).

However, all of his teaching and miracles were not the ultimate drawing power. After Jesus rose from the dead, he appeared to hundreds of people during the forty days preceding his ascension to heaven (1 Corinthians 15:3-8). In spite of everything he had said and done, only 120 followers were assembled in Jerusalem awaiting the coming of the Holy Spirit and the inauguration of his earthly kingdom. However, when the death, burial and resurrection were preached for the first time after they became reality, 3,000 were baptized. On a daily basis, people were then added to the Lord (Acts 2:41, 47). Clearly, the death of Jesus had far more impact than did his teaching and miracles. Death produces fruit. In that sense, death became him, and death becomes us.

## Death Becomes Us
### Death Removes Selfishness

Selfishness is our most pervasive sin. From the cradle, it comes as naturally as the hiccups. It is such a part of our character that only the refining fires of God in our lives can expel it from our hearts. Death, in the form of self-denial, is to come at our own hand. It is a choice we each must make. However, we need motivation from above to make that difficult choice. At certain times in our lives, the motivation must be strong enough to seem like death itself. Even Paul, the master surrenderer, still needed such reminders.

> We do not want you to be uninformed, brothers, about the hardships we suffered in the province of Asia. We were under great pressure, far beyond our ability to endure, so that we despaired even of life. Indeed, in our hearts we felt the sentence of death. But this happened that we might not rely on ourselves but on God, who raises the dead (2 Corinthians 1:8-9).

Self-reliance was a temptation for the talented apostle Paul, and it took repeated reminders from the Lord to keep him God-reliant. These reminders were often severe ones. Whatever his thorn in the flesh was, he didn't want it and prayed repeatedly for its removal. But God convinced Paul how much he needed the thorn:

> But he said to me, "My grace is sufficient for you, for my power is made perfect in weakness." Therefore I will boast all the more gladly about my weaknesses, so that Christ's power may rest on me. That is why, for Christ's sake, I delight in weaknesses, in insults, in hardships, in persecutions, in difficulties. For when I am weak, then I am strong (2 Corinthians 12:9-10).

Although Paul was convinced on this occasion, other reminders were given all through his life to strongly encourage him to keep making the choice to die to self. As fellow humans with Paul, we need no less, and thankfully, God will provide no less.

Paul wrote three passages in Galatians that teach fundamental lessons about destroying selfishness. The Christians in Galatia were quite worldly, which is to say, quite selfish. In Galatians 4:19 he wrote, "My dear children, for whom I am again in the pains of childbirth until Christ is formed in you...." From his own example, he taught that Christ cannot be formed in us until we are crucified with him:

> I have been crucified with Christ and I no longer live, but Christ lives in me. The life I live in the body, I live by faith in the Son of God, who loved me and gave himself for me (Galatians 2:20).

Then, in Galatians 6:17 he showed that crucifixion with Jesus included serious suffering: "Finally, let no one cause me trouble, for I bear on my body the marks of Jesus." The way of the cross was the only way home for Jesus, and it is the only way home for us. Surrender cannot be watered down. God loves us enough to keep applying the pressure needed to keep us choosing self-denial.

## Death Matures Us

Death to the selfish self is the only antidote for childishness. While *childlikeness* is a required spiritual characteristic (Matthew 18:2-4), *childishness* is a decidedly unspiritual quality. Self-denial must be consistently applied to uproot the latter from our nature. Jesus was tempted with selfishness just as we are. Each of the temptations Satan offered after the 40 days of fasting was addressed to the self: feed yourself; prove yourself; and reward yourself (Luke 4:1-13). After Jesus prevailed over these temptations, Satan left, but only "until an opportune time." Temptations, by their very nature, appeal to the self. Therefore, death to self is a continual necessity.

Without this death, we cannot mature into the image of Christ. If he could not be perfected for his role as Savior of the world without suffering—in spite of being sinless— then we should not expect less. One of the most informative passages on the subject is Hebrews 5:7-10:

> During the days of Jesus' life on earth, he offered up prayers and petitions with loud cries and tears to the one who could

*save him from death, and he was heard because of his reverent*
*submission. Although he was a son, he learned obedience*
*from what he suffered and, once made perfect, he became the*
*source of eternal salvation for all who obey him and was*
*designated by God to be high priest in the order of Melchizedek.*

The loud cries and tears of Jesus were not simply those
associated with the last night in the Garden of Gethsemane.
They occurred during the "days" of his life. These times of intense
struggle were a part of the process of training him to be a high
priest. This role demanded total selflessness, to be sure, but it
also demanded a total focus on the needs of others. It demanded
sympathy *and* empathy.

The text says he was heard because of his reverent submission.
In what sense was he heard? Although the One to whom he
prayed was able to save him from death, that One did *not* save
him from death.[2] Jesus' prayers were surrendered to the will of
the Father, aimed at meeting the needs of others rather than his
own. In that sense, he was clearly heard, and the prayers were
answered. But the answers did not consist in deliverance from
the struggles; they consisted in perfecting him for the task of
saving and serving others. He was already perfect in sinlessness,
but not in preparation. Having suffered, he can totally identify
with us in our temptation struggles. Therefore, he is the perfect
high priest.

We are likewise perfected, or matured, in our "death-to-self"
battles if we approach them in the right way. Any person with
inner strength and determination can endure some tremendous
pressures for a short while, maybe even for an extended period
of time. But if he looks at the struggle in only a humanistic way,
once it ceases, he has gained little toward developing a Christ-
like character. Therefore, the Bible admonishes us to keep a godly

---

[2] *Ek* in Greek here translated "from" can be translated "out of," and in
that sense, God did save him "out of" death—i.e. did not leave him in the grave.

perspective of the trials we face. Paul rejoiced in them (2 Corinthians 12:10), and challenges us to do the same (Romans 5:3-5). Incredibly, James wrote,

> *Consider it pure joy, my brothers, whenever you face trials of many kinds, because you know that the testing of your faith develops perseverance (James 1:2-3).*

All such trials must be met with a death to self if we are to benefit from them. We can simply set our jaws and endure them, but we will gain little. In all tests, we must look for the hand of God and for the lessons he is attempting to teach us.

Surrender at such times means that we avoid two extremes. In a context dealing with divine discipline, the writer of Hebrews defined these two extremes with these words:

> *"My son, do not make light of the Lord's discipline,*
> *and do not lose heart when he rebukes you,*
> *because the Lord disciplines those he loves,*
> *and he punishes everyone he accepts as a son"*
> *(Hebrews 12:5-6).*

What does it mean to make light of the Lord's discipline? Simply this: to explain it in humanistic terms instead of looking for the hand of God in it. On the other side of the coin, we cannot look at the discipline and think God is down on us. Our tendency is to take discipline (in whatever form) as a negative rather than as the positive which the Bible asserts it is. Looking for God's lessons in spite of our pain accomplishes his purposes, and we are thus matured.

One day, after we had been in Boston for several years, I was feeling frustrated. In the course of discussion with my wife, I wondered why my ministry had to be as hard as it seemed at that point. She replied, "Your biggest problem spiritually is pride and mine is fear. God brought us here to be disciplined and trained in these areas." I felt much better immediately. What she said rang true, and once I could see the hand and plan of God in the challenges, I was relieved. Suffering for no reason has never appealed to me at all, but suffering for God's refining of my character appeals greatly. If we understand the purposes of the challenges, they actually affirm the love God has for us.

God not only has our best interests at heart; he will not be moved off his course to break us, mold us and mature us. He has no sentimentality about him. We can weep and wail all we want, but he will not quit giving us what we need rather than what we want. Many times I have complained and begged for a particular cup to be taken from me, only to later thank him for not listening! As the writer of Hebrews put it,

> *No discipline seems pleasant at the time, but painful. Later on, however, it produces a harvest of righteousness and peace for those who have been trained by it (Hebrews 12:11).*

Death to self produces maturity. Therefore, we need to view discipline for what it actually is—a "word of encouragement" (Hebrews 12:5)!

## Death May Not Always Remain Symbolic

As we discuss cross-bearing and death to self, it is important to remember that for nearly all of the apostles and for thousands of Christians in the early centuries of the church, the death was not symbolic. Perhaps we then can face our challenges with a lighter spirit and more grateful heart. As the Hebrew writer stated in Hebrews 12:4, we have not yet resisted to the point of shedding our blood. But many of our early brothers and sisters in Christ did reach that point. Listen to the words of Jesus:

> *"Brother will betray brother to death, and a father his child. Children will rebel against their parents and have them put to death. All men will hate you because of me, but he who stands firm to the end will be saved" (Mark 13:12-13).*

> *"All this I have told you so that you will not go astray. They will put you out of the synagogue; in fact, a time is*

*coming when anyone who kills you will think he is offering a*
*service to God" (John 16:1-2).*

The threat of physical death is already a part of following
Jesus in certain countries. As Americans become more godless
and more aggressive in their godlessness, we cannot believe we
will be exempt from bodily harm. If I understand Revelation 20
correctly (and I'm not dogmatic about it), Satan at some point
will be released from his present restrictions and duplicate a
situation similar to that in the infancy of the church. A part of
his deception of the nations relates to the persecution of the
church. That worldwide persecution was brought about by the
worldwide proclamation of the gospel. Our accomplishment of
Christ's mission today carries the risk of bringing disciples face-
to-face with the certainty of physical persecution. Are you ready
for such? Not unless you are surrendered to Jesus. Discussing
theory is intellectually challenging; putting it into practice is
downright sobering.

### Death Blesses Others

The death/life principle reaches its pinnacle in the impact it
has on other people. It was in Jesus' suffering and death that he
became most attractive and had the most impact. Everyone suffers
and dies, but his suffering and death were uniquely different.
His was focused on blessing others with redemption. Because of
that focus, he suffered and died far differently than others in
similar circumstances. Others who were crucified screamed at
their crucifiers with hatred; Jesus said, "Father, forgive them."
Others only thought of their own pain; Jesus only thought of the
needs of those around him. Mere suffering accomplishes little,
but *redemptive* suffering changes lives forever.

An old hymn has this stanza in it, "Must Jesus bear the cross
alone and all the world go free? No, there's a cross for everyone,
and there's a cross for me." Why is there a cross for everyone?

Because all who live godly lives will be persecuted? Partially, but much more is at stake. Crosses result from persecution, and they are a part of character refinement. However, their greatest purpose, as with the cross of Christ, is redemptive. When we suffer *with a surrendered spirit*, we attract and impact like Jesus. We thus become Jesus to the world.

One of the most important passages in helping us understand the redemptive nature of our suffering is 2 Corinthians 4:7-12, which reads as follows:

> But we have this treasure in jars of clay to show that this all-surpassing power is from God and not from us. We are hard pressed on every side, but not crushed; perplexed, but not in despair; persecuted, but not abandoned; struck down, but not destroyed. We always carry around in our body the death of Jesus, so that the life of Jesus may also be revealed in our body. For we who are alive are always being given over to death for Jesus' sake, so that his life may be revealed in our mortal body. So then, death is at work in us, but life is at work in you.

This passage points out how suffering affects us (moves us to rely on God) and how it affects others. The life of Jesus is most apparent in us at the precise times when his death is apparent in us. His life, with its impact on hearts, shines brightest through us when we are suffering with Christ-like attitudes. The essence of those attitudes is our *willingness* to suffer that others might be drawn to him.

In Philippians 3:10-11 Paul gives us more insight into how this works:

> I want to know Christ and the power of his resurrection and the fellowship of sharing in his sufferings, becoming like him in his death, and so, somehow, to attain to the resurrection from the dead.

Knowing Christ and his resurrection power demands our sharing in his sufferings and becoming like him in death. The deepest communion with Jesus can never be enjoyed until we have imitated him in redemptive sufferings.

The last passage we will consider in this vein is Colossians 1:24:

> *Now I rejoice in what was suffered for you, and I fill up in my flesh what is still lacking in regard to Christ's afflictions, for the sake of his body, which is the church.*

At first reading, it seems incredible that Paul would claim something was lacking in Christ's afflictions. Did not Jesus say on the cross, "It is finished?" Do not the Scriptures affirm repeatedly the all-sufficiency of his suffering on Calvary? *Yes*, to both questions. However, Paul's words are not at all ambiguous—something was lacking! What was that "something"?

Jesus was the *fullness* of God in bodily form, says Colossians 1:19 and 2:9. This means that he was a demonstration of God in the flesh. According to the Gospel of John, one major purpose of the Incarnation was to show man what God was actually like. John 1:18 says, "No one has ever seen God, but God the One and Only, who is at the Father's side, has made him known." Further, Jesus said to one of his apostles, "Don't you know me, Philip, even after I have been among you such a long time? Anyone who has seen me has seen the Father. How can you say, 'Show us the Father'?" (John 14:9). The point is that no one could fully understand God until they saw him in human form.

Now, let's take this line of reasoning one logical step further. Not only was Jesus the *fullness* (demonstration) of God; the church is the *fullness* of Christ (Ephesians 1:23)! Colossians 2:9-10 ties both concepts together: "For in Christ all the fullness of the Deity lives in bodily form, and you have been given fullness in Christ, who is the head over every power and authority." Paul prayed that each disciple would be filled with the fullness of God (Ephesians 3:19). Although no individual is the fullness of Christ, if each of us is filled with God through the Holy Spirit, then the composite body of Jesus (the church) is the fullness of him (Ephesians 4:13).

God's wisdom is obvious. If he could not be really understood without being perceived in the flesh through Jesus, then Jesus also cannot be really understood without being seen in the flesh— *our* flesh. The world must see us loving and serving as did Jesus during his earthly sojourn, but more is needed. If it took a cross to draw the world to Jesus originally, it will still take a cross to draw them. And unless people see a cross borne in the lives of his followers (his *fullness*), they will not be drawn to him.

Do you grasp the magnitude of what it means to deny self, take up a cross daily and follow Jesus? The implications are *staggering*! We have the obligation as disciples to imitate the extraordinary life of Jesus, and to take his message all over the world. But we also have the obligation to take his death all over the world in our bodies—we must demonstrate his cross to the world by being lifted up in *our* suffering, maintaining surrendered, godly attitudes in the process. When death to self becomes a reality in our lives, then, and only then, can the life of Jesus be demonstrated in our mortal bodies. We must humbly realize that *we must die to bear fruit!*

# CHAPTER 8

# Entrusting Ourselves to God

laves, submit yourselves to your masters with all respect, not only to those who are good and considerate, but also to those who are harsh. [19]For it is commendable if a man bears up under the pain of unjust suffering because he is conscious of God. [20]But how is it to your credit if you receive a beating for doing wrong and endure it? But if you suffer for doing good and you endure it, this is commendable before God. [21]To this you were called, because Christ suffered for you, leaving you an example, that you should follow in his steps.

> [22]"He committed no sin,
> and no deceit was found in his mouth."

[23]When they hurled their insults at him, he did not retaliate; when he suffered, he made no threats. Instead, he entrusted himself to him who judges justly. [24]He himself bore our sins in his body on the tree, so that we might die to sins and live for righteousness; by his wounds you have been healed. [25]For you were like sheep going astray, but now you have returned to the Shepherd and Overseer of your souls (1 Peter 2:18-25).

## Trusting God When Life Is Unfair

Suffering for doing good with a surrendered spirit under the sovereign hand of God is the call and the challenge. The idea sounds noble, but in many specific situations, our souls revolt against doing it. A friend told about a woman he knew—I will call her "Linda"— who was facing such a challenge. Her immediate superior in her job was leaving the position, and the vacancy was scheduled to be filled with someone already in the department. Two women were named as candidates for the promotion, including Linda. The other woman wanted the position badly and had no scruples about how she obtained the promotion. Therefore, she began to slander Linda (who was very spiritually minded). Knowing what was happening, Linda decided to obey 1 Peter 2 and go the way of the cross.

Finally, the day arrived and the promotion was announced. The job went to the unrighteous rather than to the righteous. That seems terribly unfair, doesn't it? It was, but then God never promised us fairness in the world. His Son certainly did not receive fairness at the hands of his world. On the first day in her new position, the slanderer triumphantly entered her new office, only to receive a big shock. On her desk was a bouquet of flowers from the one whom she had mistreated so shamelessly, and a note which said something like this: "Dear _____, Congratulations on your promotion. I pray that your new job will be a joy to you. If I can help make it better in any way, please allow me to serve you in whatever way I can." As she read the note, she broke down weeping and then called Linda in to beg for her forgiveness.

When we hear a story like Linda's, we have two strong but conflicting feelings well up inside us. One, we feel admiration for the spiritual woman who went the way of the cross. Two, we still struggle with the feeling of righteous indignation and the sense of unfairness. The struggle intensifies considerably if we are the one facing the challenge of unfair treatment. However, Jesus left us an example to follow in such cases. His righteous indignation came into play when he was defending the Father, but never in self-defense. He did not retaliate when attacked, choosing rather to entrust himself to a loving God. And now, we are called to follow in his steps.

The Golden Rule was memorized by many of us when we were small children. It sounds so nice, but demands so much:

"Do unto others as you would have them do unto you." In the context of 1 Peter 2, it demands that a slave who is being treated horribly respond with genuine respect for his harsh master. His response is not *reaction* to his earthly master; it is *action* toward his true Master, Jesus. Anyone can act nicely to those who treat him nicely. Only a Jesus-imitator can act nicely in the face of rudeness and ugliness. Read carefully Jesus' words in Luke 6:27-36, keeping in mind that these are not pious platitudes to be admired, but principles to be lived daily:

> "But I tell you who hear me: Love your enemies, do good to those who hate you, bless those who curse you, pray for those who mistreat you. If someone strikes you on one cheek, turn to him the other also. If someone takes your cloak, do not stop him from taking your tunic. Give to everyone who asks you, and if anyone takes what belongs to you, do not demand it back. Do to others as you would have them do to you.
>
> "If you love those who love you, what credit is that to you? Even 'sinners' love those who love them. And if you do good to those who are good to you, what credit is that to you? Even 'sinners' do that. And if you lend to those from whom you expect repayment, what credit is that to you? Even 'sinners' lend to 'sinners,' expecting to be repaid in full. But love your enemies, do good to them, and lend to them without expecting to get anything back. Then your reward will be great, and you will be sons of the Most High, because he is kind to the ungrateful and wicked. Be merciful, just as your Father is merciful."

The personal example of Jesus shows us what true godliness is. It includes not retaliating in the face of ill treatment, but it goes far beyond a refusal to strike back. He acted positively in all cases in order to soften the hearts of his accusers. As Romans 5:8 puts it: "But God demonstrates his own love for us in this: While we were still sinners, Christ died for us." The way of the cross calls for love in response to hate; kindness in response to ruthlessness; and acceptance in the face of rejection. Later in Romans, Paul calls us to imitate God in demonstrating love for our enemies:

> Do not repay anyone evil for evil. Be careful to do what is right in the eyes of everybody. If it is possible, as far as it depends on you, live at peace with everyone. Do not take revenge, my friends, but leave room for God's wrath, for it is written: "It is mine to avenge; I will repay," says the Lord. On the contrary:
>
> > "If your enemy is hungry, feed him;
> >     if he is thirsty, give him something to drink.
> > In doing this, you will heap burning coals on his head."
>
> Do not be overcome by evil, but overcome evil with good (Romans 12:17-21).

Some of us have a stronger sense of fairness than others. In many ways, this quality is godly and helpful. However, if it is not tempered by an understanding of the lessons in this chapter, it can cause us to avoid surrender. The idea of fairness should be pursued conscientiously by every disciple in his treatment of others. On the opposite side of the coin, we should not have high expectations of fairness to be shown us. A part of the problem is that our definition of fairness may be biased, thus setting us up to over-react to what we presume to be unfair treatment.

More importantly, an expectation of always receiving fair treatment is neither practical nor biblical. Life is not fair. Facing unfair treatment with a surrendered spirit gives us the opportunity to demonstrate the life of Jesus in a powerful way. The way of the cross leads us to a number of actions; accepting unfairness with a smile is one of the most powerful.

## Trusting God When Righteousness Brings Rejection

Persecution for the follower of Christ is most often verbal and emotional rather than physical. However it comes, it is not easy to accept gracefully. Rejection hurts. But it is a part of the Christian life. Light and darkness have never mixed well and never will. Paul wrote: "In fact, everyone who wants to live a godly life in Christ Jesus will be persecuted" (2 Timothy 3:12). Both the reasons for persecution and the sources from which it comes are quite varied.

Persecution is similar to a snowball rolling down a hill—it gains size and momentum once it begins. Jesus himself was widely acclaimed and accepted in the early stages of his ministry. However, his life and teaching eventually prompted those in the darkness to kill him. Similarly, the early church experienced an early acceptance followed by a progressive rejection. The favor they enjoyed in Acts 2:46-47 soon gave way to the persecution of apostles in Jerusalem (Acts 4:16-20; 5:27-29, 40-42), the persecution of other disciples in Jerusalem (Acts 8:1-3), then in other parts of the world (Acts 17:5-8). Finally, it reached the point that Jewish leaders in faraway Rome would say "people everywhere are talking against this sect" (Acts 28:21-22).

The message of Jesus and discipleship is threatening to people, and often their persecution of the messengers springs from this fact. Family ties are threatened by the call to put God first (Matthew 10:34-37); false teachers and false teachings are threatened by the proclamation of truth (1 Timothy 1:3-4; 2 Timothy 4:2-4); business and financial success are threatened by commitment to righteousness (Acts 19:23-34); and those pursuing worldly pleasures are threatened by those living a pure life (1 Peter 4:3-4). Righteous reactions to persecution begin with righteous attitudes. We should not be *surprised* when it happens (1 Peter 4:12-16) and must keep in mind that it could be much worse (Hebrews 12:2-3). Because suffering for righteousness' sake has the potential of drawing people to Christ, as well as changing our own character, we should always rejoice in the anticipation of God's reward (Matthew 5:10-12).

When our attitudes are godly, our actions will be also. These actions include a refusal to give in to fear and back off from our convictions, while continuing to be gentle and respectful toward those who persecute us (1 Peter 3:14-16). We must simply make sure we are suffering for doing good and not for some sin. Then we must keep trusting God and doing what he said (1 Peter 4:19)!

Disciples cannot expect the world to view them positively, either as individuals or as a collective group. The news media makes a living by attracting an audience with sensational stories. Combine this motive with their lack of understanding about the spiritual realm, and you have the necessary elements to prompt misrepresentations on a broad scale.

Years ago, I remember reading adverse publicity about the group of which I am now a part. Many of my friends and relatives reacted with alarm. My initial reaction was quite the opposite. The churches of which I had been a part for years attracted little attention from the world. In general, they were considered respectable and acceptable in their communities. I often wondered just why we were not viewed and treated like Jesus and the early church. The answer should have been obvious. We were not hurting Satan's cause enough to prompt him to stir up the world against us. The presence of persecution does not prove that a person or group is of God, since it is possible to be persecuted for unrighteousness or for righteousness. But the *absence* of persecution makes a clear statement about the lack of godliness. In my case, adverse publicity caused me to take a closer look in order to determine the reasons behind the publicity. I simply refused to allow any man or group of men, no matter how "respectable," to do my thinking for me. My search led me behind the false accusations to a group of surrendered disciples, loving

God and other people, dedicated to Jesus' mission of seeking and saving the lost.

If Jesus and his early followers were misrepresented and downright slandered, we should not be taken aback when the same thing happens to us. Nor should we be shaken when otherwise well-respected members of the community are the ones doing the damage. It was the *establishment* who nailed Jesus to the cross, and the religious leaders who demanded it. In our world of traditional religion, most people have been inoculated against the real thing. Therefore, the genuine article is going to be seen as strange and treated accordingly. Trust God and respond in harmony with his teachings on the subject. Even when the world thinks we are weird, God applauds our faith and our bearing of the cross. Relax and rejoice!

## Trusting God When Husbands Are Overbearing

The way of the cross explained in 1 Peter 2:18-25 is continued in chapter 3. (Keep in mind that chapter and verse numbers were not originally a part of the text.) When Peter turns his attention to wives and husbands, he has not changed subjects. His use of the phrase "in the same way" makes this point clear. With the concept of surrender in view, consider his admonitions to wives in chapter 3:1-7:

> *Wives, in the same way be submissive to your husbands so that, if any of them do not believe the word, they may be won over without words by the behavior of their wives, when they see the purity and reverence of your lives. Your beauty should not come from outward adornment, such as braided hair and the wearing of gold jewelry and fine clothes. Instead, it should be that of your inner self, the unfading beauty of a gentle and quiet spirit, which is of great worth in God's sight. For this is the way the holy women of the past who put their hope in God used to make themselves beautiful. They were submissive to their own husbands, like Sarah, who obeyed*

*Abraham and called him her master. You are her daughters*
*if you do what is right and do not give way to fear.*

The subject of a wife's submission to her husband's leadership
is a sensitive one in our society. The sensitivity is due to an
incorrect understanding of what is and is not entailed in the
definition. Certainly no "dictator" mentality, with its
accompanying harshness, is a part of God's definition. However,
our cultural problem goes beyond definitions—one of the fruits
of the feminist movement is rebellion against authority.
Submission has not been tried and found to fail; it has been
found difficult and gone untried.

Surrender is at the heart of biblical marriage, but it tests the
spiritual commitment of both women and men in a profound
way. The male/female marriage roles discussed in the latter part
of Ephesians 5 really starts with verse 21: "Submit to one another
out of reverence for Christ." According to the verses following
this one, the woman is to submit to the leadership of her husband
and the man is to submit to meeting the needs of his wife.
Submission, with its necessary component of surrender, is not
simply for the wife. Every human relationship is predicated on
the same principle demanded in following Jesus. Love of God
and of neighbor must follow the same path.

The home is one of the best laboratories for the testing of
surrender and servanthood. We may be the best of servants to
others besides our mates, without being servants to them. We
find it easy to "let down" with our spouses, but answer the phone
or the door with a very different demeanor. God and our children
are seeing these evidences of a lack of surrender and submission,
no matter what may remain hidden from the rest of the world.
And we are earning from God the odious title of "hypocrite."

But back to the text in 1 Peter 3—a wife, following Jesus and
the way of the cross, is "in the same way" to be submissive to her
husband with all respect. Her submission is not to be conditional,

that is, based on his leading in a righteous manner. If he is not obeying the word of God, she must. Even if he is supposedly a Christian and is disobedient, she is to respect and obey. The passage is not simply speaking of non-Christian husbands. The final verse urges her not to give in to fear. What is the fear? Being afraid that submission will cause her to be run over by a disobedient, harsh husband. Peter says that she must, as did Jesus, entrust herself to God who judges justly.

I remember reading a story about a religious woman whose husband was not religious and was very difficult to live with. She asked advice of a minister, who told her, in essence, to surrender and confess to her unspiritual husband the sinful attitudes in her own heart that were hurting their marriage. She bristled with indignation and replied, "I will not. He is the problem in our marriage, and I will never accept the blame."

The minister answered, "Well, you have to make the choice of how to respond, but my advice is still the same—surrender."

After a long sleepless night, the woman came to the breakfast table to find her husband hidden behind the newspaper as usual. At some point, he growled, "What did you learn last night in your little religious meeting?" She then went to his chair, got down on her knees, and said, "I learned that our marriage problems are my fault."

To her amazement, he almost knocked the table down getting down on his knees, confessing, "No, I'm the one to blame. It's all my fault."

They ended up trying to out-apologize each other, and that's not a bad problem to experience!

Of course, our humanism kicks in about right now and reacts against the woman accepting the blame when the husband was likely more at fault than she. The issue is never "Who is the most at fault?" The issue is surrender and acceptance of personal responsibility for not following Jesus' example in bearing the cross. In the story, the woman was the only one professing Christ. She had much more responsibility before God, because she had signed on to follow Christ. In this case, she did exactly what Peter by inspiration was requiring—surrendering and trusting God with the ultimate outcome. Wives, are you doing the same? Are you willing to repent and begin doing it? If your answer is "No" for whatever reason, you are not responding as a disciple of Jesus.

The woman in the illustration learned a valuable truth about how to change your mate. Peter said to clothe yourself with righteousness and thereby win over your husband without nagging. I remember trying to counsel a Christian woman with a non-Christian husband. He was clearly a challenging person, to put it mildly. But she had tried for years to change him with incessant fault-finding. In the midst of the counseling session, I finally asked her why she had persisted in this approach for nearly two decades, with no success to encourage her. Her reply? "I guess I thought at some point it would finally work." Amazing! Her approach may seem natural when faced with living in a marriage like hers, but it can never work because it is at odds with the principles of God.

A better example is a story (fictitious, I assume) of a woman who followed a different route with her husband. She asked advice of a professional counselor about how to hurt her husband in the deepest way possible. She was fed up with him and the bad marriage they shared. The counselor advised her to be everything he wanted in a wife for six months—wear the clothes he liked, cook the food he liked, clean the house the way he wanted, and make love in his favorite ways. Then, after six months when he would have fallen back in love with her, she could walk out on him and destroy him! The idea appealed to her greatly, and she left the counselor's office vowing to follow the plan exactly.

About a year later, the counselor saw her in a grocery store, and went over to speak with her. He asked how the plan had worked.

"What plan?" she replied.

"You know—the one to make your husband fall madly back in love with you and then to walk out on him."

The woman looked at the man in disdain and said, "Mister, do you think I'm crazy enough to walk out on the best husband in the world?"

The woman had discovered the truth that mates cannot be changed directly by us; they are only changed indirectly. As we change, they will change. Both the Bible and life's experiences agree on this point. The way of the cross is the only way to escape the ungodly, unhappy ways of the world's marriages.

Not every unbeliever will be won over by a righteous wife. In some cases, the attitudes of the non-Christian may grow even worse. However, the disciple must rejoice that she is doing the right thing and following in the steps of Jesus Christ, whether her husband responds or not. In some way, God will use her righteousness and surrender to impact the lives of others.

## Trusting God When Wives Are Perplexing

Husbands are not left out of Peter's admonitions, although their need to surrender may not be as apparent at first glance. After all, the wives are to submit to them! Notice what Peter says about the challenges of the husbands: "Husbands, in the same way be considerate as you live with your wives, and treat them with respect as the weaker partner and as heirs with you of the gracious gift of life, so that nothing will hinder your prayers" (1 Peter 3:7).

"In the same way," begins Peter. Which way? The way of the cross, doing the spiritual things rather than the natural things. The most important principle in the passage is for the husbands to be considerate and respectful of their wives. The King James Version translates "be considerate" as "dwell with them according to knowledge." In other words, the godly husband is expected to consider and understand the needs of his wife and to meet them.

The challenge is that men are usually prideful enough to think they are always right, especially in the way they look at life and make decisions about life. In this condition, they are not given to being considerate or respectful. They may look at their wives and think (or say): "How can anyone think like that? Why are you like you are? It just doesn't make sense!" Pride, pride and more pride. Husbands, who designed and created females? You could have done a better job, you say? (Actually, you only *think* it, don't you?!)

Earlier in our marriage, I marveled at the male/female differences between Theresa and me. Some of these differences were funny, and some were not at all funny. Some produced laughter, and others produced anger and tears. We reasoned differently, among other things. I would come to conclusions based on the *obvious* facts (my opinion). She would not have the answers to my 14 points of stellar logic behind my conclusion. She was more intuitive and would often say something like this, "Well, I cannot answer your arguments, but I feel your conclusion is wrong." In the early days, such an answer infuriated me. If you cannot answer my "logical" arguments, how can you reject my conclusion?

The wife, according to Peter, is the "weaker" partner. In what ways is she weaker? Not spiritually or intellectually. Physically in most cases, and to some degree, she is usually more fragile emotionally. Certainly in dealing with crises of health and family, she may be stronger emotionally. But her design makes her more sensitive emotionally. Men are often out of touch emotionally with themselves, their wives and their children. God designed a woman to complement a man in his tendency to be ignorant of this realm. Of course, the worldly-minded man prides himself on being "tough" rather than "emotional." However, he is very unlike Jesus in this area and is actually fearful of experiencing the deepest of feelings. This fear explains his reluctance to be vulnerable and real with others around him. Through his pride and fear, he is duped by Satan into thinking he is tough when he is actually a wimp.

No, husbands, your wives are not like you. They are not supposed to be. In the beginning, God made male and female. Neither is complete without the other. You may be stronger in some ways, but according to Paul in 2 Corinthians 12, you can never be strong until you accept your weaknesses. And you do have plenty of them, the biggest of which are pride and selfishness. These worldly sins come out most in the way you treat your wife. The challenge of the cross is to love her unconditionally, which includes studying her as a person and meeting the needs she has whether those needs make sense to you as a male or not.

Thankfully, I have learned to appreciate and trust the differences in my wife (usually!), especially her intuitiveness. If she does not feel good about major decisions we are making, I back off and look further at the situation. Through the years, I have been spared some tragic mistakes by trusting her sensitivity. She is different from me in many ways. Praise God, for I need all the help I can get!

At this point, we should not have to remind husbands that our responsibility before God is to meet the needs of our wives whether they are angels or wretches. True righteousness does not depend on the other person. Pick up your cross, Mr. Strongman and show some *real* strength. Plainly and simply, just be like Jesus. Serve, serve and serve some more, even when your service may go unnoticed and unappreciated. Trust God and be righteous, for in doing this, others will see Jesus in human form and may then be healed by your wounds!

# CHAPTER 9

# Biblical Principles in Action

*nd what more shall I say? I do not have time to tell about Gideon, Barak, Samson, Jephthah, David, Samuel and the prophets, who through faith conquered kingdoms, administered justice, and gained what was promised; who shut the mouths of lions, quenched the fury of the flames, and escaped the edge of the sword; whose weakness was turned to strength; and who became powerful in battle and routed foreign armies. Women received back their dead, raised to life again. Others were tortured and refused to be released, so that they might gain a better resurrection. Some faced jeers and flogging, while still others were chained and put in prison. They were stoned; they were sawed in two; they were put to death by the sword. They went about in sheepskins and goatskins, destitute, persecuted and mistreated–the world was not worthy of them (Hebrews 11:32-38).*

Biblical principles remain only ideals if they are limited to the realm of the intellect. They become realistic as a lifestyle when they are filled out with flesh and viewed in life settings. The use of modern-day examples helps us see the relevance of living out these principles, but looking at biblical examples provides us with the greatest inspiration possible. The Bible is full of tremendous illustrations of surrender in the lives of its characters, those ancient men and women who chose the ways of God in spite of unbelievable challenges. An entire book could easily be devoted to these examples.

For our purposes, I have selected four biblical figures to examine because of their level of surrender.

The selection was purely subjective on my part. If someone else were writing this chapter, he or she would likely select different characters. At a different time, I would probably vary the selection. But these four have astounded me, impressed me and inspired me. When we make a serious attempt to enter their world and see things through their eyes, they come to life before us, filling us with wonder and conviction. If they did what they did without the understanding of Jesus we enjoy, we should be all the more eager to imitate them. It would be *scary* to stand behind one of these people on Judgment Day unless we had learned from them and imitated their faith!

## Abraham: Father of the Faithful

Abraham is called "father of the faithful" for good reason. He had a faith by which all others are measured and tested. Hebrews 11:8-19 lists a number of occasions when Abraham submitted to the will of God with a trust that surpassed his experiences. Actually, faith on our part is never totally blind faith—God always gives us some evidences for our faith. But then, in spite of the evidences, he will push us to our limit and demand a "leap of faith." He provided Abraham with experiences which built his faith, but then he called Abraham to make some quantum leaps of faith.

The story begins with God's call to Abram to leave his relatives and homeland. He "obeyed and went," according to Hebrews 11:8, indicating an obedient heart behind his obedient actions. He surrendered his desire to know what lay ahead. With no travel plan, no time schedule, no hotels reserved, and no housing secured in the town of his undisclosed future residence, Abraham obeyed and went. We speak of disciples being willing to go anywhere, do anything, and give up everything. It's a nice statement, but Abraham was more than *willing* to do those things— he did them *repeatedly* for 100 years (from the time God called him at age 75 until he died at 175).

Abraham was also surrendered materially. He lived in tents, rather than in a nice house, and convinced his wife to accept that same lifestyle. When the herds had grown too large for him and Lot to remain together, he gave Lot the choice of the best land. Many so-called Christians operate their business ventures with the philosophy of "God helps those who help themselves" as they grasp for complete control. The father of the faithful put the matter in a younger man's hands, trusting that his future was really in God's hands. As Hebrews 11:10 says, "...he was looking forward to the city with foundations, whose architect and builder is God." A materialistic man he was not. Although God blessed him with wealth, he would have given it up in a moment.

Abraham also was surrendered in family matters. Romans 4:19-20 states: "Without weakening in his faith, he faced the fact that his body was as good as dead—since he was about a hundred years old—and that Sarah's womb was also dead. Yet he did not waver through unbelief regarding the promise of God, but was strengthened in his faith and gave glory to God." When God informed him that his descendants would be as numerous as the stars of heaven, he believed it, in spite of his advanced age. The timing was in God's hands. He waited on the Lord, Sarah became pregnant, and the son of promise finally made his appearance.

In my mind, the high-water mark of Abraham's faith came some years later when God commanded him to sacrifice this beloved son. In Genesis 22:3, it says "early the next morning" Abraham set out on his journey to kill Isaac. *Amazing!* If I had been he, I would have postponed the whole process as long as possible. But not Abraham. He *searched* for reasons to trust God. In our logical humanism, we often look for reasons *not* to trust. Note in Hebrews 11:19 that "Abraham reasoned that God could raise the dead, and figuratively speaking, he did receive Isaac back from death." The Bible does not call his response "faith" specifically, because biblical faith is based on the word of God (Romans 10:17), and in this instance, God *did not tell him* what the ultimate plan was.

However, Abraham clung to two fundamental truths from God. One, he knew Isaac was the son of promise through whom his lineage would multiply. Two, he knew God had commanded his death. From a human perspective, the situation made no sense at all. A sermon based on this event could be titled "When God Contradicts God." But Abraham reasoned with a childlike trust that he would kill his son, and then God would simply raise him from the dead. In spite of the monumental challenge of killing one's own son, the man took it in stride because nothing in his life was held back from God. His surrender was absolute. The Lord's verdict in the matter? "Now I know that you fear God, because you have not withheld from me your son, your only son" (Genesis 22:12). James added this postscript to the record about Abraham: "...and he was called the friend of God" (James 2:23).

## Joseph: When Sight Is Limited

Joseph was surely one of the finest heroes in the Old Testament. "Surrender" could have been his middle name. It all started with dreams—dreams which neither he nor his family could understand. Yet, his brothers were jealous of him, and ultimately sold him into slavery. Can you imagine what he must have felt as a 17-year-old? Forsaken by family and by God, or so it might have seemed to an ordinary man.

But Joseph was no ordinary man. He held on to God, not because of any evidence that doing such paid dividends, but because of personal faith and integrity. Others would have been weeping and questioning God in the extreme, while Joseph went about doing his best for God. As soon as his pursuit of excellence seemed to be yielding its just rewards and he was promoted in his master's house, the bottom fell out. Refusing to compromise his morality because of his commitment to God, he was falsely accused of attempted rape. Do you grasp what his refusal to commit immorality really meant?

Joseph had gone for *years* without the influence of family or spiritual fellowship. It would have seemed to most people that God had forsaken him. As a young man, his natural passions would have been at their peak. Surely the possibility of sexual activity would have cast an alluring spell on him! And yet, what was his heart in the matter? "How then could I do such a wicked thing and sin against God?" (Genesis 39:9). He had received no spiritual encouragement or direction besides the convictions he gained as a boy growing up in a Hebrew home. Now far from that home and its influences, he maintained purity for his God, even though no human was looking over his shoulder to check up on him.

After being thrown into jail for refusing to violate the law of God, he had a choice to make. He could either become faithless and bitter, or spend himself in pursuit of excellence. Amazingly, he stayed the course with God in spite of having absolutely no spiritual influence outside his own faith. No church service, no Bible, no righteous fellowship—nothing! But just as he had been promoted to run his master's house, he ended up running the jail in which he was a prisoner. Cream always rises to the top. But another major disappointment was on the way.

Joseph interpreted dreams for two men, one of whom should have remembered him after being set free. However, he apparently became sidetracked by the joy of his release and did not remember to work for Joseph's freedom. Surely Joseph would now begin to question the God who was allowing all of these injustices! If he did at all, it wasn't for long. He was sold out for God, with a faith based not on reward, but on surrender alone.

Sold into slavery at age 17. Jailed for doing good. Forgotten by a man who owed him his life. Approaching age 30 after 13 long years of frustration and disappointment. Tempted to blame it all on God, and retreat into self. Yet, Joseph held on to God. He became better, not bitter; more faithful, not less; dedicated, not doubtful; righteous, not resentful. The result? Besides the 13 years of ill treatment? He ended up ruling the greatest nation the world had ever known at that point in history, and in the process, saved his own family through which God was to bless the world. During all of the difficult years, he was not campaigning for the vice-presidency of Egypt. He was not aware the office was up for grabs. He only knew that God was God, whether times were grand or grueling, and he held on for dear life.

Our patience with God is put to the test with the passage of 13 days, and *severely* tested in 13 months. The thought of patiently waiting on God to act for 13 years is *overwhelming*! How long does it take you to lose faith and give up on God? Without the Bible, without fellowship, without physical or spiritual family, how would you have done? How well are you doing now with the benefit of all of those things? It is one thing to serve while looking for return benefits; it is quite another thing to serve when the benefits turn to ashes. We have much to learn from Joseph. When sight is limited, only faith sustains.

Why do you serve God? What benefits do you hope to receive? How much are your dreams tied to personal recognition and accomplishment? The *Joseph principle* of rewards is based on doing right with or without rewards. Do your best, and trust God to do his best. Serve because you love him, and give him free rein to do with you what he thinks best. Joseph did not serve to gain promotions; he served only to please his God.

The Hebrew writer was dealing with this same principle in Hebrews 13:5 in directing us to be content with what we have. Joseph was more content than we could imagine. How does the principle relate in our setting? The army captain should be content with his rank, if he is a disciple of Jesus. He should not be serving for the purpose of being promoted to the rank of major. He should serve as though he were serving Jesus. If and when he does receive a promotion, it must come as a by-product of serving his true Master.

The same application may be made to any employment promotion or raise in salary. Disciples must work for God, not for promotions or raises. The principle most definitely applies to advancement in the kingdom of God, as well. If you do what you do spiritually in hopes of "advancing" in leadership, you are already on the devil's track. You had better start imitating Joseph and simply doing your best for God without regard for advancement. Then God can advance you, knowing you will give him the glory rather than keeping it for yourself. The *Joseph principle* is a vital one—don't miss it!

**Daniel and Friends: No Compromise**

Every Bible story book devotes space to Daniel in the lion's den and to his three friends in the fiery furnace. Their courage is legendary. Behind that courage was their surrender to the God of heaven. Daniel 6 tells how his righteousness was noticed by the king of Babylon, who was intent on placing him over the entire kingdom as chief administrator. True to worldly form, his fellow administrators were threatened and envious of his favor with the king; therefore they devised a plan to discredit him. They attempted to get the king to agree to throw any person into the lion's den who prayed to anyone besides the king for a 30-day period. He agreed, and the stage was thus set to remove Daniel from the scene.

Death penalty or not, Daniel was no compromiser. Three times a day he prayed to God in a room with open windows. As expected, his enemies were watching and brought his disobedience to the king's attention. Although the king did not want to enforce the penalty, he felt obligated to obey his own law and had Daniel thrown to the lions. Of course, we are familiar with the miraculous intervention of the Lord, leading to Daniel's preservation and the destruction of his enemies (Daniel 6:19-24).

Surrender is shown in Daniel's refusal to compromise in order to save his own life. He could have prayed silently or privately, but he prayed in a room with open windows. He was not ashamed of his God, nor inclined to hide his love for him. When he prayed, he not only asked for help in the serious situation that he faced; he also thanked God as he had always done (Daniel 6:10). Hysteria did not enter his heart to erode his faith. His attitude was one of complete trust in God.

How easily we back down from being public with our faith! We may feel self-conscious about praying in public places before meals or talking of spiritual things openly. Our cultural setting generally stands opposed to public manifestations of one's faith. Keep it inside church buildings, and all is well. Announce it for all to hear, and many are offended. Inviting strangers in the marketplace to spiritual activities seems *weird* in the eyes of the majority of people, even religious ones. Coming out in the open with our faith will cause negative reactions, but it will not cause us to be thrown into a den filled with lions. On Judgment Day, suppose that you follow Daniel in facing your Maker. What will be your rationalization for having kept your faith private in too many instances? Surrender to God and timidity about God are not traveling companions. It all boils down to faith in, and love for, our eternal Friend.

Next, consider the account in Daniel 3 of Shadrach, Meshach and Abednego in the fiery furnace. Similar to Daniel's challenge with the later king, Darius, they faced an edict issued by King Nebuchadnezzar to worship a golden image he had set up. They refused, and he reacted violently and pridefully to their refusal. He had them brought before him for a personal confrontation. With a blood pressure level high enough to test the outer limits of a sphygmomanometer, the king made his threats. Knowing of their faith, he concluded his threat with this sarcastic comment: "Then what god will be able to rescue you from my hand?" (Daniel 3:15).

Can you picture the magnitude of that moment? Royalty lined up to watch the show. The king, determined to intimidate these young Jewish lads. The foreboding sights, sounds and smells. However, all of these physical trappings were ineffective in threatening men of God who had surrendered hearts. They were unfazed. Rather than being intimidated, they became the intimidators. Their refusal to compromise or beg for mercy is etched in history as one of the most courageous statements of faith on record:

> Shadrach, Meshach and Abednego replied to the king, "O Nebuchadnezzar, we do not need to defend ourselves before you in this matter. If we are thrown into the blazing furnace, the God we serve is able to save us from it, and he will rescue us from your hand, O king. But even if he does not, we want you to know, O king, that we will not serve your gods or worship the image of gold you have set up" (Daniel 3:16-18).

Their trust in God was flawless. They realized he was the King of kings and the Lord of lords. Therefore, they knew Nebuchadnezzar was a mere man who was like "a drop in a bucket...worthless and less than nothing" in the words of another prophet (Isaiah 40:15, 17). They had no defense and needed no defense, for God was their King. They had total confidence in God's power to save them from any fire stoked by man. But they also were surrendered to death if death was the will of God. Come what may, there would be no compromise of spiritual convictions on the part of these three.

Do you see the relationship between surrender and courage? Since fear is one of our most controlling emotions, we must learn from these four Hebrew wise men. A friend was speaking recently to her young daughter about inviting her schoolteacher to church.

The girl is very spiritually minded for her age but was struggling with the pervasive fear of rejection. Young or old, we feel its tentacles reaching around our hearts in all the wrong places at all the wrong times. Her mother used an illustration which made the point and produced strong convictions in her daughter. As I listened, I felt more than convictions—I felt shame about my own failures to stand up courageously and publicly for God.

The illustration went something along these lines: Imagine that your friends at school loved to be around you most of the time. But, when other people came up who were not a part of your close group, your friends would have nothing to do with you. Then, once the others left, they immediately came back around you and resumed the close association and relationship. How would their turning away from you make you feel? If they were ashamed of you when others were present, would they really be friends at all?

*Good questions!* Especially when you make the spiritual application to our relationship with Jesus. Do you love to be around him, talking and rejoicing with him, until others who don't know him or like him come around? Do you then get embarrassed and look the other way until they leave? And once the comfort zone is restored, then you can get back to enjoying your Friend? Suppose on the Judgment Day you stand beside Shadrach, Meshach and Abednego as you face the Judge?

My purpose is not to put anyone on a guilt trip. Rather, I want all of us to see the power of a surrendered faith. When we are sold out to God, believing and feeling that his love is better than life itself (Psalm 63:3), we will find the conviction and courage to stand up for God like never before. These four men from the past were but flesh and blood like we are. What they did, we can do. What they refused to do, we can refuse as well. Surrender and compromise are diametrically opposed, but surrender and courage are inseparably joined. Surrender, get a gleam in your eye, and imitate the faith of these young Hebrews!

## Mary: Reputation Sacrificed for God

"Mary, the mother of Jesus." An exalted title, is it not? But in her lifetime, she had a shoddy reputation among her peers. From the day she became an expectant mother, her reputation was sacrificed for God. The account in Luke 1 describes the angel's visit to Mary, informing her of the plans for her to bear a unique baby. Again, the key to appreciating the story is to put yourself back in her time.

Mary's first shock was produced by the appearance of the angel. That experience alone produced a flush of adrenaline into her system. Next, she is informed about the upcoming birth of her holy child, the God-man Jesus. Now we are talking about super-shock! She was asked to contemplate the unthinkable, the unimaginable, the indescribable. "How," she asks, "as a virgin?" "By the power of the Holy Spirit," the answer comes, "as he overshadows you" (whatever that may have involved). Do you understand the answers? Then neither did she! The passing of centuries have not lessened the mystery. Mary was asked to accept the fact of the virgin birth and the presence of God in her womb, both of which she was incapable of understanding.

Her reply reflects pure, untarnished surrender: "'I am the Lord's servant,' Mary answered. 'May it be to me as you have said'" (Luke 1:38). Beautiful; delightful; inspirational! No wonder God had her prophesy "'From now on all generations will call me blessed'" (Luke 1:48). She had remarkable faith guarded by a childlike simplicity. But life would test her faith at the moment her belly began to swell. The self-righteous religionists of her day were not gracious about infractions of their law. Immorality was punishable by death, according to that law.

Of course, you and I know her condition was caused by God. But what do you think her peers thought about her story? "Oh, I see. You're still a virgin, are you? God caused your condition, did he? Sure we believe you; it happens like that all the time, doesn't it? Just last year, young Martha over in the next town gave birth to God, and now it's your turn! He will just shrink down and crawl into your womb, no problem!" The ridicule must have been *enormous* in scope. However, being pregnant out of wedlock was a small matter compared to the claim of being pregnant with a God-child. But that was her story, all of her life. Remember that only a minority in the Jewish nation ever accepted Jesus, and in Nazareth the percentage appeared to have been much smaller than in other towns. Mary sacrificed her reputation for God, no doubt about it.

What is the application for you and me? As humans, we are saddled with two strong aversions which relate to this lesson. One, we dislike conflict and become expert conflict avoiders. Two, we want desperately to have approval from others and thus become people pleasers. Mary couldn't run and she couldn't hide. She had to face the conflict and live with the fact that the approval of men would be out of the question for her. She stood out in the crowd—everyone knew her name and her story. She most likely was the focus of many off-color jokes and had to learn to live with the derision.

How do you handle being viewed as an overzealous "Bible-banger"? What do you do with the negative view those in our world have of the truly committed? We are not discussing how to be religious without really trying, or how to be part of a socially acceptable little church. We are discussing being a follower of Jesus Christ. Who was he? In heavenly terms, he was God in human form. In earthly terms, he was the radical, revolutionary leader of a youth movement. The apostles were most likely younger guys. If John wrote Revelation and his gospel when tradition says he did, he would have been a teen during the ministry of Jesus.

Older people in biblical times were not substantially different from older ones now. In my experience, the majority of people develop hardening of the *attitudes* even before they develop hardening of the *arteries*. Only the young or the young at heart have the idealism to enlist in a cause which brings rejection and slander. The church I was a part of as a young married was unusual in its day, for it had many younger members. However, a visit there now brings visions of white hair with few youths in sight, which is sad. Sad because youths are no longer shown the challenge of following the real Jesus; and sad because the older members have lost their idealism. Of course, I have nothing against age *per se*, since I am presently 52 years old. But I have much against the tendency of the older generation to soften the demands of Jesus while fighting to maintain the *status quo* of traditional, comfortable religion!

Jesus did not walk the green hills of Galilee verbalizing nice little spiritual adages that would be suitable for greeting card inscriptions. He incited a spiritual revolution against the views of the religious establishment of his day. And his work got him killed as a criminal! *That* is who you are following if you are a disciple. My concern is that many of the young zealots among us get married, have children, embark on careers, and ultimately become a part of the establishment whose values they once rejected in favor of following Jesus. In biblical terms, they lose their first love and become lukewarm (Revelation 2:4; 3:15-16). A major part of the problem is their desire for the kind of reputation which neither Jesus nor Mary ever had.

Our heroes Abraham, Joseph, Daniel, Shadrach, Meshach, Abednego and Mary laid it all on the line for God—their reputations and their lives. Are you willing to do the same? Our society is not that different from theirs. We somehow think it is, but it only *seems* different because God-followers today are different. We don't take the same risks nor do we call others to face up to the God who will judge them. We find it all too easy to practice a respectable style of religion rather than the style which causes the battle lines between light and darkness to be clearly seen and clearly drawn. Surrender is not simply a nice way to discover how to have an inner feeling of peace and tranquillity. It is God's extremely challenging approach to living and proclaiming the Prince of Peace to a world who has lost interest in his style of religion. If God were writing his book about our generation, would you be a key figure in it? You could be. The stuff of which heroes are made is still available. Let's imitate the surrendered faith of those ancients of whom the world was unworthy, and make a similar impact on eternity!

PART

# Surrender:
# The Practicals

# CHAPTER 10

# Are You Surrendered?

One of the difficulties in having a faith that surrenders is that we can think we have it when we really do not. Another difficulty is that we can be surrendered at one point, and then gradually take control back from God. Just *when* we cross over that line is not always easy to recognize, primarily because the change is a gradual one. And there is also the possibility of a *partial* surrender: the surrender of one part of life while maintaining control of another part.

Perhaps total surrender is a rare commodity, even among Christians. However, we must all grow in it as fast as possible. The only thing that will really satisfy the soul's deepest needs is a growing personal relationship with the Creator of our spirits, and we cannot have that growth without surrender. For those who are willing to "let go and let God," there is a sort of fourth dimension available to us, full of peace and power. It enabled Jesus to face a cross and change the world, and it will enable us to do the same.

But now, how about the question of whether you are surrendered or not? How can you know for sure? Your answers to the following questions will help you to accurately assess your level of surrender.

## How Do You See the Person in the Mirror?

Our first question concerns your self-esteem. Everyone struggles in one way or another at one time or another with his or her self-image. I have never met anyone who was exempt from the struggle. However, the sad truth is that most of us wrestle inwardly with how we feel about ourselves far too much. The number of books written on this subject, with and without a Christian perspective, attests to the scope of the problem and the interest people have in it. Surrender to God is the antidote for low self-esteem.

In an earlier chapter, I mentioned a book entitled *The Rejection Syndrome*. One of the key tenets of that book is that our low self-esteem, or insecurities about ourselves, come from the rejection we have received in life. As might be expected, the rejections which have the most impact on us are those experienced early in life from our most significant relationships. Without question, parents are the biggest players in life's game of forming the self-image.

In his book, Solomon divides rejection into two basic types: overt and covert. The overt type is obvious and recognizable to even the casual observer. The covert type often is not. However, both types are just as damaging. Overt rejection comes when parents convey a lack of desire for their child or a lack of love. (For instance, "You were an accident, you know." "We really wanted a girl when you were born." "Your older sister is easy to love, but you certainly aren't.") Covert rejection comes in many forms. The death of a parent or the divorce of parents often make a young child feel rejected. Even "smother love" is covert rejection, because the child is controlled to the point he is not allowed to be his own person.

When rejection has made its mark on our emotions, we develop insecurities about ourselves, and our self-esteem suffers. We then start reacting in unhealthy and ungodly ways in our attempts to offset our feelings of insecurity. These wrong reactions are closely related to how we view two significant areas in our lives—performance and people.

When we see proper performance as the way to self-esteem, we often react in two very different ways. We may avoid trying to perform because we fear failure. Or, we may "over-perform" because of that very same fear. In the former case, we withdraw into the shadows and avoid risks; and in the latter case, we keep trying to "prove" our worth to ourselves with accomplishments. But success in performance only alleviates our feelings of inadequacy temporarily, and soon we are back on the treadmill of trying to prove ourselves.

A number of years ago, I remember reading a magazine article in which highly successful people shared their fears of being "found out." Although they were visibly successful, they felt like impostors in a sense. Inside, they still felt inadequate and also felt that they did not belong in the position they were in. Therefore, they lived with a sense of dread about being exposed for who they really were (as they saw themselves). No matter what our accomplishments may be, we will not feel good about ourselves on the basis of performance because of the haunting threat of future failure.

Our view of other people also has great impact on our self-esteem. If we are trying to have our need for significance and security met by people rather than by God, some tough times await us. We become overly concerned about what people think about us and always seem to be on a program of proving ourselves to them. But men or women cannot give us ultimate security and significance—only God can. A person who is secure in his relationship with God (through surrender) can be a people *server* rather than a people *pleaser* or a people *impresser*. Most of us are far too concerned about how others may view us. Jesus, our role-model, was only concerned about how God viewed him.

Even when we see clearly that our need for self-esteem is to be met in Christ rather than by people, our security with God must be based on his *acceptance* and not our *performance*. We can be guilty of trying to earn our standing with him, which gets us right back into the same cycle we may have been in with people. We must not *do* in order to *be*, but rather *be* in order to *do*

(Ephesians 2:8-10). A surrendered person has a healthy view of his own sinfulness and constant need for grace, understanding that he works not to be saved, but because he is already saved. The confidence he gets from God's acceptance overcomes his feelings of insecurity. He thinks correctly about himself because of who he is in Christ, and that leads to healthy feelings of self-esteem.

A word of caution is in order here. Understanding grace does not by itself settle our hearts regarding the performance issue. We are created so that our hearts will be at peace only when we are surrendered and sold out to God. If we are mistaught how to accept significance and security in Christ, we will often feel as though we are not measuring up. But on the other hand, if we are unsurrendered, our consciences will continue to plague us no matter how well we have been taught. Like a race car engine, we have been designed to run at a high rate of RPM's for Jesus, and if we continue running at low throttle, we will become full of all kinds of spiritual "sludge."

How we feel about ourselves is tied directly to how we think God feels about us. Unless we are able to throw off our "prove-it," "earn-it" or "measure-up" mentalities with people and with God, we will remain on a performance treadmill. Our feelings about ourselves must be based on the understanding expressed by the little boy who said, "God made me, and God don't make no junk." While his grammar may have been lacking, his theology was right on target. Our value comes from the fact that we are created in God's image, and the price paid by the death of his beloved Son absolutely establishes our worth. Accept his view of you and be content, or reject it and be miserable. The person in the mirror will never look good to you until you see your value biblically, but that view will never register in your heart until you are surrendered to Jesus' lordship. How surrendered are you? Start out by answering the question about your present level of self-esteem.

## Pepped Up or Pooped Out?

A second consideration in determining whether we are surrendered or not involves our energy level. All of us often have to function with less energy than we would wish, and if we have a health limitation, the challenge becomes more acute. However, a low energy level can be an indication of a spiritual problem. In this case, if we are working in our own power rather than in God's power, we will become tired much more easily than we would otherwise. At issue is how we face the challenges of life for God.

All of us have learned to *behave* spiritually to one degree or another. But is that behavior action or reaction? In other words, are you acting out the part (in which case you will tire easily), or has your behavior become a result of the Spirit dwelling in you?

Some years back, I attended a men's retreat in a very serene camp setting. My part on the program was minimal. Therefore, I looked forward to the retreat as a time of rest and relaxation. Such was not my experience, for I returned home tired. When I expressed surprise to Theresa about my tiredness, her reply hit home. She suggested that I was still wearing my "minister's demeanor," acting out the role rather than relaxing. I was an unsurrendered performer without realizing it at the time. It takes work to *act* but much less work to *be*!

In Galatians 5:16-25, Paul describes spiritual behavior—first, what it is not (verses 19-21: the acts of the sinful nature), and then what it *is* (verses 22-23: the fruit of the Spirit). If we are "gutting it out" in either fighting sin or promoting righteous actions, our success will be short-lived and shallow. "Are you so foolish? After beginning with the Spirit, are you now trying to attain your goal by human effort?" (Galatians 3:3). Apart from Christ we can do *nothing* (John 15:5)! Surely one who is crucified with Christ and now has Christ living in him (Galatians 2:20) will be relaxed enough to enjoy his Christianity.

Being God's child must be seen as something we *are* rather than as something we *do*. For example, evangelism should be the natural outgrowth of a Spirit-filled heart. God works from the inside out. The mouth speaks from the overflow of what is really inside us (Luke 6:45). God must create in us a new heart, but he can only do that when we surrender to him and let him in to perform the necessary surgery.

When we really *are* spiritual, rather than simply spiritual *actors*, we will live life differently. Yes, Christians will still get tired, but the tiredness will be that of satisfaction rather than stress. And yes, we will tire more easily with age, but we will accomplish great things by God's power, and we will have the satisfaction of *wearing out* instead of *rusting out*. The surrendered person will experience more *energy*, more *accomplishment*, and more *exhaustion*, but the exhaustion will be accompanied by a warm inner glow of satisfaction rather than an inner turmoil of frustration.

### Do You Live in Romans 7 or Romans 8?

A third evidence of our current surrender quotient concerns our frustration level with our spiritual life. One of the most frustrated religious experiences described in the whole Bible must be that in Romans 7:14-25. Here Paul describes someone with a spiritual *understanding* and a spiritual *motivation*, minus the spiritual *power* to carry through. "I do not understand what I do. For what I want to do I do not do, but what I hate I do...What a wretched man I am! Who will rescue me from this body of death?" (Romans 7:15, 24). No wonder his frustration caused him to cry out in desperation!

But just who was Paul describing in this passage? Many would assume that he was speaking of himself as a *Christian*. It is true that he is using both first person and present tenses. It is also true that all Christians are involved in a spiritual warfare in which the Spirit and flesh are in opposition to each other (Galatians 5:17). However, a closer consideration of Romans 7 in context would suggest that Paul was describing his former life as a Pharisee in a very graphic way for the purpose of convicting others (even Christians) who were still afflicted with self-reliant attitudes.

The Jews of the first century were immersed in a "do-it-yourself" approach to religion. They were very self-righteous on the conscious level (see Luke 18:9-14), but Paul's words would indicate that in their heart of hearts, there must have been a repressed frustration.

In Paul's case this frustration may have played a major role in his hatred of Christ and Christians. However, the Damascus road experience lanced the wound and the inner anguish surfaced. Baptism into Christ had to wait for three days of spiritual self-examination. He couldn't become "Paul" until he got in touch with "Saul."

Romans 7 seems a classic attempt to help works-oriented people to recognize their own misplaced confidence in the flesh and to be ready to accept God's gracious answer in Romans 8. Because of that, the lessons of this passage apply perfectly to any works-oriented, unsurrendered person today. When a Christian begins to feel the same frustrations described in Romans 7, he can be sure that he is losing his grip on grace and he is regressing into "works." A comparison of the specifics in this passage with other clear biblical teaching will demonstrate that disciples should not be burdened by such frustration.

Romans 7 does not describe the normal Christian life as God intended it. For example the man of Romans 7 was said to be under bondage to sin, whereas he should be in bondage to Christ (Romans 6:16). Furthermore, he *practiced* sin, whereas the Christian *practices* righteousness (1 John 3:7-9). Sin indwelt the man of Romans 7, but Christ indwells the Christian (Galatians

2:20). The frustrated man had good intentions but was unable to follow through. The Christian *can* follow through with God's power (1 Corinthians 10:13; Philippians 2:12-13, 4:13). In Romans 7, the flesh was winning the struggle between flesh and Spirit; in Romans 8, the Spirit was winning. "The law of the Spirit frees us from the law of sin and death" (Romans 8:2—compare with Romans 7:23). The Christian is filled with rejoicing (Philippians 4:4), not with wretchedness (Romans 7:24).

No, Christians should not be examples of the frustration described in Romans 7. When the Father, Son and Spirit dwell in us, we have enough power to do immeasurably more than we ask or imagine (Ephesians 3:14-20). Deep frustrations in our lives are indicative of an *unsurrendered* heart. We have wandered back into the desert of self-sufficiency described in Romans 7. We are trying to operate by our own power rather than by God's. He loves us and wants to enjoy marvelous fellowship with us, but we must let him in. He stands with patience and love, knocking on the door of our hearts (Revelation 3:20), but the knob is on the *inside* only. You must open it up and let him in, and that calls for surrender. Will you do it?

## How Tightly Are You Wound?

Anxiety is a fourth indicator of our level of surrender. An anxiety-ridden person is both *prideful* (thinking no one can run things except himself) and *unsurrendered* (believing God himself can't handle it). Paul's admonition in Philippians 4:6-7 is a command and not simply a suggestion:

> Do not be anxious about anything, but in everything, by prayer and petition, with thanksgiving, present your requests to God. And the peace of God, which transcends all understanding, will guard your hearts and your minds in Christ Jesus.

We are forbidden to worry about anything, and the prescribed cure is surrender. In practical terms, we are to worry about nothing and pray about everything, really believing that God is in control. The result of all of this is a peace which transcends all understanding.

How high is your anxiety level? Worry is practical *atheism*. A real heartfelt trust in God will allow you to be at peace. We live in an *uptight* generation only because people do not believe in God. They may believe in *a* god, but not in the God of the Bible who can totally provide for those who are his and have completely turned over their lives to him. Thinking spiritually is choosing to focus on God's solutions instead of our problems.

In his excellent book, *Mind Change*, Tom Jones shows that even as disciples, we tend to combine faith in God with our problems in this manner: "I know the promises of God are true, *but* my problems are overwhelming." Such thinking has no power in dealing with worry. The correct order should be: "My problems may seem overwhelming, *but* God's promises are true and greater."[1] It's a matter of focus. All of us have good things and bad things in our lives. We have to make decisions about whether we will focus on the positive (and greater) aspects or the negative (and lesser) aspects. Even if we have a 90% to 10% positive-to-negative ratio, a focus on the negative will make it seem like the reverse ratio is true.

Too many of us are like a woman I met many years ago. We were talking about the old adage stating that 95% of all that we worry about never comes to pass anyway, showing the fruitlessness of worrying. She expressed her attitude toward life with the following observation: "Well, since 95% of all we worry about doesn't come to pass, I try to worry about as many things as possible. Then 95% of it will be kept from occurring!" It sounds humorous, but after getting to know her better, I realized that she actually practiced her theory fairly consistently.

All of us must be properly *concerned* about the challenges in our lives, but *not anxious* about them. The difference between

[1] Jones, pp. 50-56.

concern and worry is that concern moves us to address the situation and put a plan into action, whereas worry simply *worries*! Someone once described the difference between a psychotic person and a neurotic person in these terms: a psychotic honestly believes that 2 + 2 = 6, and if you listen to him explain it long enough, he may convince you of it. A neurotic knows that 2 + 2 = 4, but it *worries* him! Too many of us have a lot in common with the neurotic. We put a premium on worrying, and the result is that we are controlled by our anxieties instead of our faith in God. Are you surrendered? How high is your anxiety level?

**Afraid or Assured?**

Another surrender gauge is our fear level. Fears are actually intensified anxieties. When we don't deal with our worries, they will turn into fears which grip our hearts and control our actions. Various fears can plague us, but two of the biggest in the hearts of many are the fear of death and the fear of Judgment. The former type is often found in an exaggerated concern about potential health threats. Another word for the problem (besides faithlessness) is "hypochondria." I can personally attest to the damage caused by this malady, having experienced it for a number of years.

When I was still a teen, I began a cycle which has followed me through much of my adult life. The cycle began with a time of unusual stress in my life, which then resulted in a physical symptom as the stress made itself known in my body. In the next part of the cycle I would focus on the physical phenomenon rather than the situation causing the stress. Like a dog chasing his tail, the problem then had no solution and the physical ailments worsened. My imagination has at times conjured up the fears that I had any one of a number of dreaded diseases, from heart trouble to cancer.

Looking back at some instances when I was unsurrendered and falling prey to this cycle, some of the situations were almost humorous. Satan will do anything to make you believe the scenarios in your runaway imagination; and God will allow him to do it in order to test you and to hopefully move you toward deeper surrender. I recall thinking I had some particular disease, and then every health article in the newspaper seemed to address it. Friends in conversation seemed always to mention the specific disease as they discussed others who were sick or dying! In those situations if the disease was not mentioned, I knew better than to ask. But I usually did, and the answer was exactly what I feared most—the malady I was worried about having!

Death is a certainty. All of us are going to die, and we had best come to terms with it before we are stricken with a terminal illness. I read about one man who purchased a coffin and began sleeping in it in order to get used to it! That is not what I'm suggesting, but we must come to terms with our mortality and surrender. Before we exited the womb, our days were already numbered (Psalm 139:16). Before the cross and the resurrection of Christ, the fear of death was a serious problem, as evidenced by this passage in Hebrews:

> Since the children have flesh and blood, he too shared in their humanity so that by his death he might destroy him who holds the power of death—that is, the devil—and free those who all their lives were held in slavery by their fear of death (Hebrews 2:14-15).

Paul's unusual experience described in 2 Corinthians 12:1-7 surely altered his view of life after death. Therefore, without the slightest reservation, he could say,

> For to me, to live is Christ and to die is gain. If I am to go on living in the body, this will mean fruitful labor for me. Yet what shall I choose? I do not know! I am torn between the two: I desire to depart and be with Christ, which is better by far (Philippians 1:21-23).

Consider also his similar statements in Romans:

*For I am convinced that neither death nor life, neither angels nor demons, neither the present nor the future, nor any powers, neither height nor depth, nor anything else in all creation, will be able to separate us from the love of God that is in Christ Jesus our Lord (Romans 8:38-39).*

*For none of us lives to himself alone and none of us dies to himself alone. If we live, we live to the Lord; and if we die, we die to the Lord. So, whether we live or die, we belong to the Lord. For this very reason, Christ died and returned to life so that he might be the Lord of both the dead and the living (Romans 14:7-9).*

As I have grown older, I am obviously closer to death than ever before, but I worry about it far less. Because of learning more about surrender and putting it into practice more consistently, my psychosomatic illnesses and my hypochondria have nearly disappeared. But when I find myself becoming preoccupied with thoughts of health, I know that my surrender level has slipped. When we are surrendered to God and his plan for our lives, we have a different perspective on eternity. Did not God say: "Precious in the sight of the LORD is the death of his saints" (Psalm 116:15)?

But what about the second source of fear mentioned earlier—the fear of Judgment Day? Surrender answers that fear as well. Listen to John's words:

*And so we know and rely on the love God has for us.*

*God is love. Whoever lives in love lives in God, and God in him. In this way, love is made complete among us so that we will have confidence on the day of judgment, because in this world we are like him. There is no fear in love. But perfect love drives out fear, because fear has to do with punishment. The one who fears is not made perfect in love (1 John 4:16-18).*

A disciple who is surrendered to God faces death and the knowledge of Judgment with boldness and confidence. But fears in these areas and others (sharing your faith, leading, financial sacrifice, etc.) clearly demonstrate a lack of surrender. What does your fear level tell about how surrendered you are?

## What's Close to the Surface?

Anger is yet another indication of our level of surrender. An unsurrendered person is often identified by his anger. He or she may attempt to repress it, but it oozes out through the pores of the skin. Since our spirits communicate on some level with the spirits of other people, our anger often can be sensed even when it cannot be seen. Although anger, in the form of righteous indignation, is not sinful. Jesus demonstrated it on a number of occasions. But such righteous anger is always aroused because of injustices done toward God or mistreatment of others and never because of things done to us.

Unrighteous anger is always ugly but particularly so in those who claim to have God in their lives. The older son in the parable of the prodigal son was an angry man. His anger teaches us a lot about ourselves and the way we view God's blessings. After he found out about the return of his younger brother and the special treatment he was receiving, he became so mad that he would not even go into the house. The father (representing God) came out to reason with him, only to hear his son say:

> "Look! All these years I've been slaving for you and never disobeyed your orders. Yet you never gave me even a young goat so I could celebrate with my friends. But when this son of yours who has squandered your property with prostitutes comes home, you kill the fattened calf for him!"
>
> "My son," the father said, "you are always with me, and everything I have is yours" (Luke 15:29-31).

As with this older son, religious people often direct their anger at God. "He is in control after all, isn't he? Why doesn't he do things in the way *I* believe to be the best?" Those are common thoughts of the unsurrendered, untrusting, unloving creatures of a loving Creator. What causes our problem? The ugly sin of ingratitude. Look at the example of that older brother. He viewed life serving his father (God) as "slaving" and "obeying orders." He was oblivious to his blessings. God told him that everything was already his! All good things are ours in Christ now, but we often choose to focus on the mundane things which are *not* ours.

I'm reminded of the poor man who saved his money for years in order to fulfill his life's dream of a cruise on a fancy ship. He finally saved the money for the ticket, purchased it, and packed for the trip. Since he spent nearly every penny for the ticket, he reasoned that he would have to take food from home and eat his meals in his stateroom. He packed the cheapest foods he could find in his suitcase, reflecting that at least he would be on the ship. Near the end of the two week cruise, a fellow passenger commented that he had never seen him in the ship's dining room. The man explained his lack of money and the need to eat canned food in his room. With amazement, the other person replied: "Man, didn't you know that the price of the ticket included three scrumptious meals per day in the fanciest dining room you could ever hope to see?"

Are you like that man? God has given you everything already, with the promise of heaven beyond. Do you get angry when life doesn't go your way? Someone commented that the size of the man is demonstrated by the size of the things which make him mad. How big are you? How surrendered are you?

## Clothed with Humility?

A final indication of a lack of surrender relates to our level of pride. Surrendered people are humble people. They have discovered an important truth—they are not God! As fallible human beings, they have discovered their need for help from others in order to be more like Jesus. Many indicators of pride could be delineated, but the way we take correction speaks volumes about our level of pride. In the world, critique is often a negative, because the motives behind it are often designed to hurt the one being critiqued; but in the kingdom of God, critique is a positive. As the Psalmist stated it: "Let a righteous man strike me—it is a kindness; let him rebuke me—it is oil on my head. My head will not refuse it" (Psalm 141:5).

Defensiveness is an unsurrendered attitude. It shows mistrust not simply of other humans, but of God. This sort of pride does not believe that God can and will work through the people he has put in our lives. And defensiveness is *not* primarily an emotional response—it is resistance to the input of others. I have known some who were able to remain quite calm when being critiqued, thinking themselves to be non-defensive because they kept their emotions in check. However, a lack of receptivity to the input is defensiveness, pure and simple.

I'm reminded of the formula in Tom Jones' book mentioned earlier in this chapter. The wrong view of God is shown by saying, "Yes, God, *but* the problems." Whatever follows the *but* is our true heart and focus. Hence, we must say, "Yes, the problems, *but* God!"[2]

I recently had the disquieting experience of trying to help another person see some things about himself. He does not take critique well, although he rejects it calmly (mistaking his calm reaction for humility). His approach was basically, "Okay, maybe there is some truth to what you are saying, *but...*" (followed by all that he disagreed with, including something about nearly everything said). A spiritual, surrendered response would go something like this: "Well, here are a couple of points from my

[2] Jones, p. 52.

perspective, *but...*" (followed by a focus on the overall *tenor* of the criticism, without becoming side-tracked by each detail).

The truth is that we do not see ourselves clearly. Others see us more clearly than we would like to admit (if we're prideful). Prideful people make a fatal mistake in this business of seeking and accepting critique. They believe a refusal to accept the view others have of them somehow makes their own view true, not only in their eyes, but in the eyes of others as well. However, defensiveness makes the point stronger, denials notwithstanding. Such people, with their denials and dismissals, remind me of the *ostrich.* They stick their heads in the sand, thus blinding themselves to the obvious, while the part sticking up is what everyone else is looking at (not the most *presentable* part)!

I know a missionary who was said to once have been a very prideful individual. He was quite resistant to the input others gave him, and since he was blessed with a very high degree of intelligence, he had no problem dismissing the critiques. Finally, he humbled out enough to wonder why others were in such agreement in the way they described his pride. He then made the decision to accept the view others had of him, asking them to point out his pride every time they saw it surface. Not surprisingly, they were happy to cooperate! The end result? He has become a truly humble man, exalted greatly by God in every way.

> *All of you, clothe yourselves with humility toward one another, because,*
>> *"God opposes the proud*
>> *but gives grace to the humble."*
> *Humble yourselves, therefore, under God's mighty hand, that he may lift you up in due time (1 Peter 5:5b-6).*

How surrendered are you? How prideful are you?

## Conclusion

As we said at the outset of this chapter, total surrender on a consistent basis is perhaps rare, even for disciples of Jesus. But since our clear call is to imitate his perfectly surrendered heart and life, we must face ourselves and deal with our lack of surrender. In evaluating our level of surrender, we must look carefully at all the areas described above—self-esteem, energy, spiritual frustration, anxiety, fear, anger and pride. Where are the glitches in your surrender? Let's be honest and let's be faithful. We can change with the help of God, and the following chapter will provide us with the practical means of doing such. Don't give up and don't give in—surrender is still the greatest blessing in our walk with God. It is not easy to find and keep, but its rewards are more valuable than gold.

# CHAPTER 11

# How Do We Surrender?

I f you are following the reasoning of this book and are genuinely wanting to live a life of biblical surrender, you may still be wondering just how to implement this idea. In many ways "Just do it!" is good advice, but many of us have been unsurrendered in so many ways for so long that we need to be shown some kind of plan. My hope is that this chapter will help you take "surrender" from the sphere of theory to the sphere of practice.

## Be Committed to Repentance

The role of repentance is highly important in dealing with any sin (and a lack of surrender is sin!). It is true that some changes fall into the category of long-range growth, but the *conviction* which produces repentance is necessary to ensure long-term growth from immaturity to maturity, from weakness to strength. Many people have physical, sexual or emotional abuse in their past which makes them prone to struggle with the whole idea behind heartfelt surrender—a *submissiveness* which trusts both God and the people he has put into their lives. But we are often far too quick to explain away a person's problems in terms of their background. While it is true that our past does affect us tremendously, whether others have hurt us or we have hurt ourselves, a repentant heart is still the key to changing.

At one point in my life, I was often swayed by the background of people struggling with sin and was inclined to be sentimental toward them. Sentimentality does not help people to change—

period! God is decidedly not sentimental. Of course, he is sympathetic and empathetic, but these qualities are not the same as sentimentality. What helped me to see the failure inherent in sentimentality was noticing individual differences in people with exactly the same past experiences. Some whose backgrounds would seem to have limited their ability to submit to authority were still very submissive, while others with the same type of background were quite unsubmissive. It finally dawned on me that the issue was not the past, but the person's *response* to it, their willingness and desire to repent.

Once we are eager to repent, surrender is fairly simple. It is mostly the *decision* to turn all that we have and are over to God for his complete control. However, looking at the practical steps to reach and maintain complete surrender will prove helpful.

## Be Committed to the Concept

Surrender is intimately connected to faith in God, but it is a double-edged sword. Its rewards sound desirable, but its demands look foreboding if our hearts are not deeply spiritual. Therefore, we must make sure that we are onboard before pushing the boat away from the shore in our venture with Jesus.

The human control center is composed of mind, will and emotions. Unless we deal with these three in the proper order, we are not likely to surrender and stay surrendered at the deepest level. Our minds must lead the process and stay in control of our walk with Jesus at all times. With our minds, we look at the biblical and practical evidences regarding the need to surrender to God. By this point in the book, you are either already convinced of the concept at the *intellectual* level, or God is going to have to take some drastic steps to convince you.

Next, we must make a do-or-die *decision of the will* to submit. Our emotions may be in rebellion, but if our wills line up behind truth, our emotions will have no option in the matter. They will fall into line as well. The thought of denying our selfish self stirs the emotions like nothing else, but we cannot give in to them. Look at the evidence, use your will to make a firm decision to do things God's way, and your emotional side will eventually conform to the correct decisions.

### Be Committed to Prayer

Begin by praying about your *decision* to surrender. Ask for God's strength to help you yield to the challenges facing you. When you feel unwilling to surrender on a given point, pray something like this: "Lord, I'm not willing, but I am willing to be made willing." Be honest about your struggles, but overcome the temptations to give in and protect self. Imitate the father whose son was demon-possessed by saying, "I do believe; help me overcome my unbelief" (Mark 9:24)! Pray, "I surrender; help me overcome my lack of surrender."

Pray also about your *fear* of surrender. Satan wants to make you fearful and mistrusting of God. He wants you to look at the concept of surrender as a way to get hurt, a way to give up control into another's hands and to be abused as a result. Always remember that God is on your side. When he must give you temporary discomfort or pain in order to help you in the long run, look for the long-range blessings coming your way. God is your Father. He delights in helping you and making you happy with a godly type of happiness. Even when you give him *carte blanche* with your life, that doesn't mean he will hurt you. Trust him, not Satan. Satan is full of deceptive lies about your need to retain control of your own life.

Pray *urgently* about your need to surrender. Quiet times with God have their place, but a cross-bearing disciple must have some *loud times*. In the OT, Jacob prayed all night, struggling with an angel of God. Note Jacob's urgency in the following account:

*So Jacob was left alone, and a man wrestled with him till daybreak. When the man saw that he could not overpower him, he touched the socket of Jacob's hip so that his hip was wrenched as he wrestled with the man. Then the man said, "Let me go, for it is daybreak."*

*But Jacob replied, "I will not let you go unless you bless me."*

*The man asked him, "What is your name?"*

*"Jacob," he answered.*

*Then the man said, "Your name will no longer be Jacob, but Israel, because you have struggled with God and with men and have overcome" (Genesis 32:24-28).*

An in-depth study of prayers in the OT is most enlightening and convicting. We read accounts of multiple men and women crying out before the throne of God with utmost urgency. People like Abraham, Moses, Joshua, Hannah, David, Hezekiah, Nehemiah and many others had prayer lives which make most of ours look like a stroll in the park. We must get a bigger view of God and the battle to which he has called us. We are soldiers in a war of unbelievable magnitude and consequences. We will never be the warriors we were designed to be without surrender; and without urgent prayer, we will never be totally surrendered!

We must pray *thoroughly* about our surrendering. At some points in our lives, surrender may come fairly easily and quickly. At other times, it will take much prayer. See it through to completion. God has tested my surrender level many times. Sometimes the testing followed great victories (as was the case after Jesus' own baptism, Matthew 3:13-4:11). Sometimes the testing came at the very difficult times (as in the Garden of Gethsemane, Luke 22:39-44). God knows exactly *how* and *when* to send these tests in order to help us discover where our hearts really are and where they need to be! Sometimes the tests come in dramatic ways and sometimes they come in ordinary ways, but come they do!

More than seven years ago, I was challenged by friends and spiritual leaders to give up the leadership of a church I dearly loved and to move across the country. They showed me my need for more training and the need to unite fully with others seeking to take the gospel around the world. These same leaders later challenged me to give up the plan to lead a mission to another city in order to remain and serve as an elder in Boston. These two dreams of mine had to be crucified for the good of the kingdom, but they did not die easily or quickly. I prayed and wept much before surrendering to those decisions. Looking back, both decisions were *obviously* the best. Frankly, surrender should have been easier in both cases in light of God's promise in Romans 8:28! The pain of surrendering to a perfect and loving God can *only* result in gain.

Some months ago, a memorable test came in a more ordinary way. Both my mother and Theresa's mother were coming up to Boston for a two-week visit to celebrate Theresa's 50th birthday. At that particular time, I was facing a writing deadline for my biggest writing project to date. As usual, I was already behind schedule! The day they were to arrive, I went out for a prayer walk. Emotionally, I felt very stressed out (unsurrendered!) and even thought to myself that writing as much as possible that day might be more important than spending time in prayer (obviously an *unspiritual* thought!).

After praying for an hour, I was still quite stressed. As I fought the temptation to give up and go back to my writing, I saw an old railroad track going through a deserted area. I immediately turned in that direction and walked down the track, praying for surrender. After another hour, I was completely surrendered and at peace with God, myself and my situation. Two weeks later, a very enjoyable visit by our mothers drew to a close and my writing was finished. More importantly, I had been calm and surrendered all during that period of time. Surrender is not simply a nice little theory—it is an amazing reality when we are determined to imitate our Master's example and to claim his faith!

## Be Committed to a Spiritual Partner

God works through people. The NT is replete with "one-another," and "each-other" passages. We serve God through serving people (Matthew 25:31-46), and God serves people through us. The church is a big family, and all of us need deep relationships if we are to grow into the image of Jesus and accomplish his mission on the earth. The discipleship described in Matthew 28:18-20 is absolutely fundamental in growing as disciples and in doing his work. Certainly something as important as surrender was never intended to be a do-it-yourself project.

A remarkable lesson about the need for close spiritual relationships can be seen by looking at an event in Paul's life. In 2 Corinthians 2:12 he informs us of a time when the evangelistic doors were opened wide for him: "Now when I went to Troas to preach the gospel of Christ and found that the Lord had opened a door for me...." If the text ended here, our imaginations could fill in the gaps of a highly fruitful stay in Troas for Paul. However, such was not the case. The next verse goes on to say: "I still had no peace of mind, because I did not find my brother Titus there. So I said good-by to them and went on to Macedonia" (verse 13).

Incredible! Paul was so dependent on the relationship with his brother that he did not take advantage of an open door provided by God! A few chapters later in 2 Corinthians, God acted in Paul's behalf in this way:

> For when we came into Macedonia, this body of ours had no rest, but we were harassed at every turn—conflicts on the outside, fears within. But God, who comforts the downcast, comforted us by the coming of Titus (2 Corinthians 7:5-6).

In Troas, the "fears within" indicate Paul was struggling with surrender but when he met back up with his brother Titus, his world came back into focus.

We must have these kinds of relationships in which we can pour out our souls to a trusted friend. Without this element, we are destined to fall prey to the closed system of reasoning mentioned in an earlier chapter and will resist surrender through our own self-deception. We are not designed to bear our burdens alone, nor are we normally capable of staying surrendered without the encouragement and direction of godly men or women in our lives. Surrender is blocked by sin, but sin is avoided by our openness not only about sins already committed but also about temptations. Surrender is promoted by righteousness, and accountability for our personal plans for growth in righteousness is essential.

Just consider a few of the "one-another" passages (with emphasis added) which show our need for relationships in order to live out the surrendered life of a disciple:

- *"I myself am convinced, my brothers, that you yourselves are full of goodness, complete in knowledge and competent to instruct **one another**" (Romans 15:14).*

- *"Submit to **one another** out of reverence for Christ" (Ephesians 5:21).*

- *"Let the word of Christ dwell in you richly as you teach and admonish **one another** with all wisdom..." (Colossians 3:16).*

- *"Therefore encourage **one another** and build each other up, just as in fact you are doing" (1 Thessalonians 5:11).*

- *"But encourage **one another** daily, as long as it is called Today, so that none of you may be hardened by sin's deceitfulness" (Hebrews 3:13).*

- *"And let us consider how we may spur **one another** on toward love and good deeds" (Hebrews 10:24).*

- *"Therefore confess your sins to **one another** and pray for one another so that you may be healed" (James 5:16).*

## Be Committed to Spiritual Challenges

Surrender requires the lordship of Jesus in our lives, and lordship requires obedience. As Jesus put it in Luke 6:46, "Why do you call me, 'Lord, Lord,' and do not do what I say?" Obeying only those commands which are comfortable and easy for us is living in our *comfort zone*. Staying in those comfort zones is diametrically opposed to carrying the cross of Jesus. We have a tendency to pick and choose what we find easiest and avoid what we find most difficult. Sometimes we even rationalize these self-serving choices with spiritual-sounding jargon, like, "That's not really my gift," or "I wouldn't want to mess it up, so I'll leave it for someone with more talent."

The NT does talk about God giving us special gifts. However, the absence of gifts in no way removes our responsibilities in the same areas. For example, Romans 12:3-8 mentions the gifts of financial giving, serving and encouraging. Those without the special gifts are not thereby exempted from financial contributions or serving others. God's plan is for those who do have the gifts to use them in such a way that those who do not have them can learn by example to serve others better. Even if I do not have the gift of encouragement, I have the responsibility of encouragement. Therefore, I need to learn from those who do it better than I do, that I might grow more into the image of Christ.

But let's go back to the need for obedience, especially in stepping out of our comfort zones to meet challenges. Such "launching out" for God stretches us and makes us more dependent on him. If our service to him is not pushing us to live on the edge for him, then we are not driven to our knees in prayer and reliance upon him. Without spiritual exercise, which strains our spiritual muscles, we will never become mighty men and women for God.

When I was in my early 20s and spiritually awakening for the first time, I learned how this principle works. The preacher often challenged us to step out on faith and not to allow a desire for comfort or a fear of failure to hold us back. All such challenges were accompanied with assurances of God's desire and ability to help us follow through. After having turned down opportunities which threatened me in one way or another, I made a monumental (for me, anyway) decision.

To make sure I wouldn't back down from the decision, I told a deacon in the congregation what it was. "For one year," I stated, "I will accept every opportunity to serve, no matter how afraid I am of doing it. And," I added, "if it doesn't work like the preacher promised, then I will leave the church." The last part was totally presumptuous, but the deacon didn't argue with me on that point. He was wise enough to know that decisions like that one would not go unrewarded by God. And it wasn't. It set my path for discovering God's radical plan for my future. At that time, I could not have fathomed what he had in mind for my life, but the catalyst for finding his plan was unreserved surrender in the form of obedience to all opportunities he put within my reach.

I read the following statement on a t-shirt: "If you are not living on the edge, you are taking up too much room!" Although the slogan was not intended to be spiritual, it is 100% accurate in describing the kind of commitment needed in serving Jesus. Nothing can be held back. When we are living with this kind of radicalness for him, we will be driven to pray like never before. And the spiritual exhilaration which accompanies surrender will charge us up to keep on keeping on, by his power and to his glory.

### Follow the Example of Jesus

Our final observations in this chapter about how to surrender come from the following example of Jesus: His greatest challenge in surrendering to the will of his Father undoubtedly came near the end of his journey to the cross. His response to that challenge demonstrates all of the above principles, showing them to be powerful in practice, and not simply impressive in theory.

> *They went to a place called Gethsemane, and Jesus said to his disciples, "Sit here while I pray." He took Peter, James and John along with him, and he began to be deeply distressed and troubled. "My soul is overwhelmed with sorrow to the point of death," he said to them. "Stay here and keep watch."*
>
> *Going a little farther, he fell to the ground and prayed that if possible the hour might pass from him. "Abba, Father," he said, "everything is possible for you. Take this cup from me. Yet not what I will, but what you will" (Mark 14:32-36).*

As we see from his example, talking about the subject of surrender is easy, but actually surrendering everything to God can be tremendously difficult. The higher the stakes, the more difficult the process. When Jesus was in the Garden of Gethsemane, he faced the most demanding decision of his life. Yet, he had a heart determined to remain surrendered to the will of God in spite of the cost involved. In one brief account, he shows us what surrender really is and demonstrates exactly how it is accomplished.

The definition of surrender is to decide to put oneself and one's future totally into the hands of God. Notice that Jesus stated very pointedly just what his desires were. But he concluded with surrender: "...not what I will, but what you will." Surrender is unconditional and total—*nothing* is held back. Jesus was struggling mightily with facing the cross, but he was determined to obey God in spite of the struggle. True surrender counts the cost of the worst scenario possible and is still willing to pay that price, if paying it is the will of God.

What do we learn from Jesus in this most difficult night of surrender? First, we see that he included other people in his prayer and in his struggle—he wanted company at such a time. Some of us are inclined to try working everything out on our own. Others of us are inclined to only talk through our challenges with others, and we do not struggle in prayer with God the way Jesus did. The former type of person lacks *humility* in self, and the latter lacks *trust* in God. Jesus lacked neither, and his prayer experience shows it. Do you tend toward one of these extremes?

Second, Jesus was totally honest with all of his feelings before God and other men. When is the last time that you told God or another person that you were "overwhelmed with sorrow"? Too many of us have far too little transparency about our lives at the feeling level. We are afraid we will appear weak or unspiritual. Again, pride is the culprit, and we need to deal decisively with this horrible sin. We are far too quick to excuse our pride (in whatever form) with the statement that "Everyone has pride." That only shows the seriousness of the problem. It in no way *excuses* it! Everyone also *lusts*. Should we therefore take *that* sin lightly? We need to get all of our emotional struggles out into the light, thereby severely limiting Satan's power in our lives (John 3:19-21).

Third, Jesus did state his *preferences* to God very clearly. Sometimes we are too quick to say, "Thy will be done." We cannot make highly difficult decisions without expressing all of our desires to God (and to others). Once we do talk out all of those desires, then we must make a decision to surrender them. But before preferences can be *crucified*, they must be *stated*. We are designed emotionally by God himself to function in this manner. He knew these spiritual struggles would be the exercise which builds spiritual muscles. And a part of that exercise is to state our desires and then reach the point that we yield them totally to God. This process was the one by which Jesus was matured for his role as high priest (Hebrews 5:7-10).

Fourth, our great Example prayed until his surrender was *complete*. He went back to his battle with prayer three times. Once he reached the totally surrendered stage, he had found the strength to face the cross and all the events which led to it. In fact, he was the only calm person in the entire chain of events because he had claimed the peace which "transcends all understanding." That peace can be claimed only by this process we are calling *surrender*, and that process cannot be completed without this kind of prayer (Philippians 4:6-7).

## Conclusion

Surrender to God is not the impossible, unreachable dream. It is attainable on a daily basis. Surrender means that we deny ourselves, take up our crosses daily, and follow him. Following him is the greatest life possible, filled with the greatest challenges possible. But follow we must, and follow we will, if we are his disciples. Set your mind on living a life of surrender and do not allow any emotion to distract you from this course. Imitate Jesus by putting the principles in this chapter into practice. Then your life will be filled with the peace and power described in Isaiah 40:31:

> ...but those who hope in the LORD
> will renew their strength.
> They will soar on wings like eagles;
> they will run and not grow weary,
> they will walk and not be faint.

PART

The God
to Whom We
Surrender

# CHAPTER 12

# God Always Knows Best

Our view of God is of paramount importance. We respond to him according to our perception of him. Therefore, if our perception is good, our feelings about him will be positive, and our responses good. If our perception is flawed, our feelings about God will be negative and our responses poor. We must develop a biblical view of him in order to love him, enjoy him and please him. And this view must find lodging deep in our hearts, not simply in our minds.

## God As You May See Him

How do we develop a view of God initially? As children, we mostly internalize the view we have of authority figures in our lives, especially parents (and more especially, fathers). If parents are lenient, we imagine that God can be manipulated in response to our self-focused whims. If parents are harsh, we believe God to be harsh and unyielding. In the parable of the talents, the third man who buried his talent viewed God as a "...hard man, harvesting where you have not sown and gathering where you have not scattered seed" (Matthew 25:24). The older brother in the parable of the prodigal son viewed his service to his father as slavery:

> "But he answered his father, 'Look! All these years I've been slaving for you and never disobeyed your orders. Yet you never gave me even a young goat so I could celebrate with my friends.'" (Luke 15:29).

Keep in mind that the Father in the parable represents God.

Once I was trying to help a friend with his view of life and religion. He tended to be harsh with those in his life, even with his devoted wife. Something was obviously amiss in his heart. Giving him biblical input always seemed to help for a while, but only for a while. He kept returning to his harmful patterns. Finally, I asked him to spend a week thinking about his view of God. I cautioned against explaining his view with biblical descriptions, because his actions demonstrated his disbelief of these descriptions. After a week he came back with two aspects of God in mind, at least two aspects as he perceived them to be.

The points he shared were these: "One, God is non-emotional, not feeling our hurts; and two, he rules by edicts—obey and be blessed, or disobey and be cursed. He is uninvolved and uncaring," thought my friend. My first response was to ask him who such a god sounded like. "My father," he replied. Knowing something about his father and his childhood, harshness would have been a nice way to describe the atmosphere and the treatment he experienced. Although his intellect was filled with the biblical descriptions of God, his heart saw God as an extension of his earthly father. With such a view, he was unhappy and often spread unhappiness to those around him.

In Romans 1:21-23, we can see that the Gentile world of the first century had reversed its definitions of God and man. Man had become, in his pride, the solution to all his problems, while God was relegated to the likeness of created things. As a result, that chapter describes the absolute depravity of those holding such distorted views of self and God. We always become like the objects of our worship. For this reason, God always hated any form of idolatry. Consider the words of Jeremiah 2:5 in this connection: "This is what the LORD says: 'What fault did your fathers find in me, that they strayed so far from me? They followed worthless idols and became worthless themselves.'"

The premise of this book is that surrender to God is not only the commanded response to him, but the most fulfilling, joy-filled response. However, unless we see God as he is, we cannot surrender to him. A flawed view of God produces fear, not security; rebellion, not submission. What about God would help us surrender everything to him? Of many depictions available, three are vital if we are to respond with the childlike faith needed. We must come to believe deeply in a God who *knows* everything, can *do* anything, and always *desires* to do the best for those he created.

## God As He Really Is

Figuring out God as he actually *is* would be impossible for mortals. Our only hope of understanding him is to see him as he has revealed himself to us in his Word. While it would be impossible for limited man to totally understand our unlimited God, he has revealed enough for us to trust him, surrender to him, and enjoy sweet fellowship with him. With that, we shall be satisfied until we are at home with him in eternity.

The Bible describes God in terms of what we normally call his "attributes." These attributes are more than qualities or characteristics. The latter two terms are descriptive of man's nature, but when applied to the nature of God, they leave a faulty impression. In the case of us humans, we have qualities which differ from one individual to another, and which also differ within the same person from one time to another. In other words, human qualities or characteristics vary in degree, and thus represent change or potential change. God does not change, and in fact, *cannot* change. He is never strong in one quality at one time and weaker in it at another. For that reason, describing him in human terminology is easily misleading. But to use the term "attribute" in depicting his nature is to recognize his unchanging essence and the fundamental difference in the Creator and the created.

A most helpful little book on this subject is *The Knowledge of the Holy*, by A. W. Tozer. He describes a number of God's attributes in a very compelling manner. This book will challenge one's thinking about God and move the reader to stand more in awe of him and his sovereignty. As we develop these last three chapters, some of Tozer's most significant comments will be included to help us in our quest for unreserved surrender to our Maker.

*He Is Perfect*

To begin with, our God is perfect. He has always been perfect and will always remain perfect. Every one of his attributes, however many there may be, is flawless and will forever be. Being perfect, he is incapable of making mistakes. Since he is absolutely perfect in knowledge, he has never learned, will never learn nor can ever learn. He is incapable of forgetting, remembering everything from the past (as we mortals term it), and knowing all things that lie in the future (as we perceive it). To God, there is no past nor future. He is the eternally existing One, who described himself to Moses with these words: "I AM WHO I AM. This is what you are to say to the Israelites: 'I AM has sent me to you'" (Exodus 3:14).

Note the following scriptures which speak of his perfection in knowledge:

I make known the end from the beginning, from
    ancient times, what is still to come.
I say: My purpose will stand,
    and I will do all that I please (Isaiah 46:10).

He determines the number of the stars
    and calls them each by name.
Great is our Lord and mighty in power;
    his understanding has no limit (Psalm 147:4-5).

Whom did the LORD consult to enlighten him,
    and who taught him the right way?
Who was it that taught him knowledge
or showed him the path of understanding? (Isaiah 40:14).

If God can neither learn nor forget, he deserves our unreserved trust. He always knows what is best for each of his creatures. If not even a little bird can fall to the ground without him being totally aware of every facet of the situation, then the tiniest aspect of our needs will never be unnoticed by him at any time, from the moment of our conception until the time of our death. He knows all there is to know about everything that can be known. He is perfect in knowledge. Trust him. Let these following words of Tozer thrill your hearts as you contemplate your perfect God.

> God knows instantly and effortlessly all matter and all matters, all mind and every mind, all spirit and all spirits, all being and every being, all creaturehood and all creatures, every plurality and all pluralities, all law and every law, all relations, all causes, all thoughts, all mysteries, all enigmas, all feeling, all desires, every unuttered secret, all thrones and dominions, all personalities, all things visible and invisible in heaven and in earth, motion, space, time, life, death, good, evil, heaven, and hell.
>
> Because God knows all things perfectly, He knows no thing better than any other thing, but all things equally well. He never discovers anything. He is never surprised, never amazed. He never wonders about anything nor (except when drawing men out for their own good) does He seek information or ask questions.
>
> God is self-existent and self-contained and knows what no creature can ever know—Himself, perfectly.[1]

## He Is Consistent

Sometimes we picture God in such a way that one attribute is said to militate against another. For example, we may describe his love and justice as somewhat of a contradiction. He loves us and wants to forgive a certain trespass, but his justice will not allow him to do it. Or, his justice is about to be satisfied, and his love

[1] Tozer, A.W. *The Knowledge of the Holy* (San Francisco: Harper San Francisco, a division of Harper Collins Publishers, 1961) 56.

overcomes his justice and allows intervention on the behalf of the sinner. Obviously, we need some help with our present comprehension of God's nature. Once again, Tozer's insights are helpful:

> God exists in Himself and of Himself. His being He owes to no one. His substance is indivisible. He has no parts but is single in His unitary being.
>
> The doctrine of the divine unity means not only that there is but one God; it means also that God is simple, uncomplex, one with Himself. The harmony of His being is the result not of a perfect balance of parts but of the absence of parts. Between His attributes no contradiction can exist. He need not suspend one to exercise another, for in Him all His attributes are one. All of God does all that God does; He does not divide Himself to perform a work, but works in the total unity of His being.[2]

Did you understand all of that? Me neither. But I understand enough to believe that my God can never be tempted with suspending his love in order to exercise his justice. In fact, he cannot be tempted to do evil in any form (James 1:13). God could never forget to show love to you or me, nor could he even choose to be unloving to us. He *cannot* make bad decisions and he *cannot* do bad things. James says he cannot even be *tempted* to do such. In working on our behalf, he never totters on the brink of indecision about which way to go. For us, decisions may fall into the right and wrong categories or into good, better or best. For God, decisions always fall into the same category—perfection, *the eternal best!* In view of who he is, we are absolutely foolish to mistrust him in any way. He is God, incapable of making the slightest miscalculation or error.

### He Is Unchanging

God is not only perfect in every attribute and perfectly consistent in those attributes, he will always be perfection. He will not change nor can he change. He will never be compelled

[2] Tozer, p. 15.

to change due to some inherent need. He has no needs. For some inexplicable reason, he has chosen to reach down and invite us into his family (praise his holy name) but he still does not *need* anything. He is perfect in and of himself. Therefore, he cannot wake up one morning with some new thought or desire which could alter the way he views and treats us. Of course, he can't wake up anyway, because he never slumbers or sleeps!

Note the following scriptures regarding this attribute of God:

*He who is the Glory of Israel does not lie or change his mind; for he is not a man, that he should change his mind (1 Samuel 15:29).*

*But the plans of the LORD stand firm forever, the purposes of his heart through all generations (Psalm 33:11).*

*I the LORD do not change. So you, O descendants of Jacob, are not destroyed (Malachi 3:6).*

*Because God wanted to make the unchanging nature of his purpose very clear to the heirs of what was promised, he confirmed it with an oath. God did this so that, by two unchangeable things in which it is impossible for God to lie, we who have fled to take hold of the hope offered to us may be greatly encouraged (Hebrews 6:17-18).*

*Every good and perfect gift is from above, coming down from the Father of the heavenly lights, who does not change like shifting shadows (James 1:17).*

Whatever God is, he has always been and will always be. Whatever he has been, he is and will forever be. Whatever he will be, he now is and has always been. He cannot change. Some people open themselves up to the possibility of believing in a changing God because of a faulty Old Testament theology. In the second century A.D., a man named Marcion depicted the OT God as being different from the one described in the NT. In other words, the God of the OT was very harsh and vengeful, but the good God of the NT (Jesus) came to save us from the wrath of the former one. Marcion was rightly treated as a heretic.

I was raised in a denomination in which a similar doctrine was espoused rather consistently. I remember hearing the Old Testament system described as a legal system, a system of "works" by which its adherents had to earn salvation. On the other hand, the NT was described as a system of grace. After all, did not John 1:17 state: "For the law was given through Moses; grace and truth came through Jesus Christ"? The contrast in this verse cannot mean that the OT had nothing to do with grace or that the NT has nothing to do with law. While the *contents* of the two covenants differed, the God who gave both is unchangeable.

If we tend to struggle with the idea of God in the Old Testament period ordering wars, capital punishment, and the annihilation of entire populations, then Marcion's doctrine may sound feasible or even appealing. But we cannot succumb to any doctrine which depicts God as varying in nature at different times. He is the same yesterday, today and forever (Hebrews 13:8). The inconsistency in the doctrine of my former church prompted me to do much study of the relationship between the testaments, which helped me to understand both law and grace far better. It was fairly simple to deduce that a pure legal system would result in either universal salvation or no salvation at all. In the first case, since everyone sins, God would have had to totally ignore his own law; in the latter case, he would have enforced it without exception. Neither case was true, because the OT was never designed as a purely legal system.

Properly understood, the salvation of people in every age has been based on the grace/faith formula. God's grace was ultimately seen in the cross of Christ. Both Romans 3:25-26 and Hebrews 9:15 tell us that faithful people *before* the cross were saved *by* the cross, because it was a reality in the mind of God before it ever occurred (Revelation 13:8; 1 Peter 1:20). Since time means nothing to God (2 Peter 3:8), he could treat a person with a right heart in the OT as forgiven before the real basis of forgiveness had actually occurred. As time-bound humans, we may have difficulty grasping this concept, but rest assured that God has no problem with it at all!

Faith is man's part, which has to do with our acceptance of God's grace. The faith conditions of accepting his gracious offers of forgiveness and sonship have varied from covenant to covenant, but in the OT or NT, salvation has always come in essentially the same way—by grace through faith. Any theology which depicts the nature of God changing in any way is bad theology and undermines our trust in the unchanging nature of our God. Whatever he was like in the OT, he is still like, and what he is like in the NT, he was in the OT as well. He cannot change, which should bring us tremendous comfort and reassurance. Tozer says it well:

> In coming to Him at any time we need not wonder whether we shall find Him in a receptive mood. He is always receptive to misery and need, as well as to love and faith. He does not keep office hours nor set aside periods when He will see no one. Neither does He change His mind about anything. Today, this moment, He feels toward His creatures, toward babies, toward the sick, the fallen, the sinful, exactly as He did when He sent His only-begotten Son into the world to die for mankind.[3]

## God As You Need to See Him

We will never understand God in his perfection. Only he is God, and only he can understand himself. But in his love and wisdom he has shown us enough to put our souls at peace from now throughout eternity. And this we need desperately to do. Trying to bear God-sized burdens even for a moment is destructively overwhelming. We need to see him for who he is and quit vying for his job!

[3] Tozer, p. 53.

Imagine yourself in the following story: It begins with me (put yourself in my place) flying on a 747 airliner over the ocean. After a nice meal, I settle in to watch the in-flight movie, comfortable and at peace with the world. About 30 minutes into the movie, the sound is cut off and the flight attendant calls rather urgently for everyone's attention to an announcement. She begins by asking if a commercial pilot is on board. Not a good beginning! I start to get nervous. No affirmative answer comes to the question. The attendant begins to explain the reason for the question and the seriousness of the situation. All three pilots ate a *contaminated* meal, and are lying on the floor violently sick. The plane is set on auto-pilot.

Next question: "Is anyone on board a private pilot familiar with flying any kind of aircraft?" Again, no affirmative answer. Now panic begins to set in. This can't be happening—this kind of stuff is for the movies! Maybe I'm asleep and having a nightmare. Time to wake up!

A third question comes: "Is anyone on board who has ever been at the controls of any kind of aircraft for any amount of time at all?" Unbelievably, no one speaks up. Finally, I raise my hand, since I have held the controls of several small single-engine planes, although I never executed a take-off or a landing.

Then, with heart pounding, knees knocking, and palms sweating, I make my way to the cockpit. Just look at all of those complex controls! What in the world can I ever do with all of this equipment? What a horrible scenario! Have you ever imagined such a situation? But there's more. Just as I drop my trembling frame down in the pilot's seat and start trying to figure out what to do, a person behind me puts his hand on my shoulder and says, "Mister, I was in the rest room while the flight attendant was explaining the problems, but I am a 747 pilot en route to my next assignment. Would you like some help?"

*Would I like some help?!* I say, "Sit down, sir, and let me get you something to drink. Then let me get out of here. I'm out of my element." I return to my seat (after my own stop at the rest room!) with my heart at rest. What a relief! I was never meant to be flying a 747. I'm just a passenger. Let the pilot do his thing and I'll do mine. Amen! Now the world has righted itself, and I'm ready to enjoy life again.

What is the point of the story? Just this: Compared to running any human's life, flying a 747 is a piece of cake. Our lives are much more complex. Yet, we try to control our own destiny and be the captain of our own fate. Why not get out of the pilot's seat and let the One who designed us direct our flight through life? We are foolish to think that we can control something as challenging as life. We are God's design, and he knows more about what we need than we could ever know. Let's wise up and realize we are not wise *enough* to do what only our Designer should be doing! Let go and let God fly your plane of life. Then you can relax and enjoy the ride, as you allow God to *be* the God of your life. Without our acceptance of an all-knowing, all-powerful, all-loving Being, we are destined for some bumpy rides and at least one fatal crash. Don't allow it to happen! With God in control the ride may still be bumpy and, at times, downright frightening, but an awesome landing is never in doubt.

# CHAPTER 13

# God Has the Power To Do Best

bout 12 years ago at an evangelism seminar, I heard a sermon by Tom Jones on the sovereignty of God that contained a memorable description of God's powerful nature. It went something like this:

> "God's sovereignty means he can do anything he wants to do, whenever he wants to do it, any way he wants to do it. He is dependent on no one. He does not answer to anyone and does not have to defend himself to anyone. God is God!"

The whole sermon was an elaboration of this idea, and its impact on my heart was staggering. Feeling physically weak, I simply remained seated after its conclusion for about half an hour. I was shown my creaturehood in a way which totally humbled me before my Maker. The feelings in my heart ranged from a righteous type of fear and trembling to a calm joy about God being God. For us to trust him, we must believe that he knows everything and can do anything.

Tozer, in his characteristically effective prose, makes these observations about this all-encompassing power of God:

> We see further that God the self-existent Creator is the source of all the power there is, and since a source must be at least equal to anything that emanates from it, God is of necessity equal to all the power there is, and this is to say again that He is omnipotent. God has delegated power to

167

His creatures, but being self-sufficient, He cannot relinquish anything of His perfections and, power being one of them, He has never surrendered the least iota of His power. He gives, but He does not give away....Since He has at His command all the power in the universe, the Lord God omnipotent can do anything as easily as anything else. All His acts are done without effort. He expends no energy that must be replenished. His self-sufficiency makes it unnecessary for Him to look outside of Himself for a renewal of strength.[1]

Once we accept the omnipotence of God, we then are faced with the dilemma of understanding why he does not choose to do everything within his potential. At the heart of this dilemma is the problem of human suffering: How do we reconcile what we know about God with what we see in the headlines of our newspapers? Skeptics, atheists and agnostics have always pointed to the problem of pain and suffering as a reason not to believe in God. Believers struggle with the same issue as they work to keep faith in God when sight seems to contradict that faith. The following section should be helpful as we grapple with this issue.

## The Problem of Evil and the Existence of God
*The Problem Stated*

The problem of why God allows evil to exist is a major hurdle to developing faith in God in the first place. Even after we come to faith, Satan will use this problem to try to trip us during difficult periods in our lives. Years ago, I read a brief but well-reasoned book by Thomas Warren entitled *Have Atheists Proved There Is No God?*[2] Although his writing is quite technical due to the use of symbolic and other formal types of logic, the basic arguments are excellent. Eventually I wrote a lesson arranging the basic arguments of that book into sermon form. The material

[1] Tozer, p. 66.
[2] Thomas B. Warren. *Have Atheists Proved There Is No God?* (Moore, OK: National Christian Press, Inc.).

in this chapter is adapted from that sermon, first presented many years ago.[3]

As we consider this issue, keep two things in mind: First, no matter how much explanation may be given, the ultimate issue will always be *faith* in the face of all storms of life. Second, while logic and reasoning cannot remove the *necessary* hurdles which faith must cross, many *unnecessary* hurdles can be taken away by practical explanations. Failure to remove those in the latter category would be a serious mistake.

Without question, one of the most challenging hindrances to believing in and trusting God hinges on the question of why he allows bad things to happen to good people, as we often phrase it. The average person would pose his question something like this: "Why does God allow disease, starvation, natural calamities, and such atrocities as war, murder, rape and the abuse of children?" The agnostic would frame his concerns more in this manner: "If God *wills* evil, he is not *good*. If God does not will evil, but it occurs *anyway*, then he is not all-powerful. Therefore, since evil exists, God must be deficient either in goodness or in power." The atheist would state his case even more strongly: "A good, all-powerful Being would *eliminate* evil completely. But, evil *exists*. Therefore, God does *not* exist!"

## Definition of Key Terms

Before we proceed, a definition of basic terms is needed. The definitions of "good" and "evil" are vital. The only true evil is what is called "sin" in the Bible, for it violates our relationship with God and with our fellowman. Conversely, the only true good is biblical "righteousness," depicting something which is *always* good, and which promotes our relationship with God and others. What we might call "instrumental evil" is something

---

[3] Due to the technical approach of Warren, my presentation represents a major rearrangement of his basic arguments. I have used material primarily from pages 32-34, 40-42, 45-50, and 67-76 of his book.

which leads men toward the ultimate wrong (sin). The things in this category can be either stumbling blocks or stepping stones, but they are not inherently evil. What we might call "instrumental good" is that which leads one toward the intrinsic good.

Thus, the same incident could be instrumentally good or bad, depending on how someone viewed it and responded to it. Sickness would be a good example of something that could be a blessing or a curse. A health problem might cause one to curse God or turn to God, depending on the heart of the person with the problem. Actually, pain itself is not necessarily evil. It may be only the symptom of a health problem, motivating a person to get needed attention, or it may be the necessary result of having obtained life-saving surgery.

The definition of some attributes of God are necessary to our understanding of the problem of good and evil. When we say God is "omniscient" (all-knowing), we are saying he knows all that is possible to know. For example, he foreknew that man would sin and would need redemption. Therefore, he created a world with that in mind, a world suitable for the spiritual development of man. Our present world was never intended to be a permanent paradise—that is reserved for *heaven!*

When we say God is "omnipotent" (all-powerful), we are recognizing he *can* do whatever is *possible* to be done. However, some things are impossible by *definition*. For example, can God make a rock too big to pick up, or a square circle? The impression left by that question is that if God had *more* power, he could. The fact is that some things are not subject to power—even God's power! He will do *only* that which is in harmony with his nature. He will not and cannot lie, for example. Nor will he interfere with the free moral agency of man. To describe God as *just* is to say that he must reward good and punish evil. Since he created man as a free moral agent, his justice requires that he allow man to make real choices.

One of the keys to understanding the problem of suffering and evil is to understand the definition of man. By God's design, man is a creature of choice, a free moral agent (and not a robot). Therefore, man can *choose* to do good or evil, even though God desperately wants him to choose good! God could not make *man* (by definition) and then refuse him the choices. (He could have made *robots* without choice, but not *man*!)

The atheist wants to know why God did not make man incapable of evil, but he is really asking why God made man in the first place (because free will is a part of the definition of man). We desire to have children, even knowing that they will make some hurtful choices. God wanted to bless us through relationships with him and with others, and you cannot have relationships if you are a robot—it's an issue of *choice*.

Another vital definition is that of our physical world. We must remember the purposes for its creation. It was designed as the ideal environment for spiritual purposes. Some of the necessary characteristics of such a world would include the following:

1. It would not just afford pleasure without responsibility or adversity (or we would all be spoiled brats!).
2. Man would be allowed the atmosphere in which to *freely* exercise choices. (Hence, some distance exists between him and God; he needs to see enough evidence of God to know that he is there, but not in a manner that overwhelms and *forces* decisions).
3. It would be suited to meeting the physical needs of man.
4. It would function in a law-abiding manner in order to teach the relationship of cause and effect. Without this feature, chaos would reign and such values as responsibility and morality could not be taught. For example, an ax is excellent for chopping trees, but it also can be used to chop people. Bricks have excellent qualities for building houses, but they

can be used to bash in someone's head. What can be done about this dual purpose situation? You cannot take away the choice from *man*, nor can you make the ax have one set of qualities when applied to a tree and another set when applied to a human! Bottom line, we must learn the law of cause and effect: Whatever we sow, we reap. And this lesson cannot be learned unless axes always cut, and bricks are always hard!

5. This world would provide *challenge* for man's intellectual powers; it would teach him to deal with obstacles.

6. Finally, such a world would need to be *temporary*, but highly *significant* with regard to the spiritual choices made in it.

*Lessons To Be Learned*

A word about the causes of human suffering is in order. True evil (sin) always comes from man's free choices. God does not want man to make such choices, and he has worked amazingly through the centuries to influence the choices to be righteous ones. One look at Jesus on the cross should be more than enough to make the point! God, however, intends that we view all challenges inherent in our temporary world with faith and respond to them in faith so that he might accomplish his purposes through them.

Things such as illnesses are a part of a temporary world, and may become instrumentally good in helping us to lean on God. Natural calamity reminds us of our frailty and serves to keep us conscious of our need for God. Some, and perhaps most, of these calamities trace back to the changes in the earth's environment after the Genesis flood—and sin caused the flood (and thus, indirectly, the changes). Some calamities today relate to what we ourselves have done to pollute and harm our environment, but the fact that we experience natural calamities is consistent with God's purpose to train us spiritually. They remind us that life is certain (in that it will end) and uncertain (in that the time of its end is unknown).

Next, let's consider the design of human suffering. God's allowance of suffering relates directly to his goal of spiritually developing mankind. Most human suffering is brought on directly by the free moral agency of man. For it to have the desired impact on our choices, it must affect us randomly. (If suffering only happened to the unrighteous, the temptation to seek God for wrong reasons would be tremendously strong!)

The benefits of suffering are multiple if we respond to our circumstances with faith in God. Suffering sets the stage for a person to live a life of self-denial, which is the greatest life possible. It affords a person the opportunity to develop his moral character (James 1:2-4; Romans 5:1-5). God can lead people to himself through suffering, either originally or later (if they have left him). It provides for a person's love to be tested in the best way possible (as in having to choose suffering over sin). Suffering can develop our compassion for our fellowman. It helps a person to better appreciate his love for God and God's love for him; his love for others and theirs for him. It will help anyone better appreciate the life to come. Finally, suffering influences others to become Christians, because they see our response to suffering to be far different from the responses of unbelievers. A cross borne courageously in our lives is still the drawing card for others (Colossians 1:24).

The proper *attitudes* to maintain as we face human suffering are based on the possible purposes behind the suffering. As we consider the several alternatives which God may be trying to accomplish in our lives, we learn the appropriate responses of faith. One, God may chasten his children in order to mold them, in which case we humbly *submit*. Two, we may suffer persecution because we are sons and daughters of God, in which case we *rejoice*. Three, we may not be able to understand just why we are suffering, in which case we *trust*. In all things, we look to the cross of Christ and see that God shared in our suffering, experienced it to the full degree and in so doing, showed us the greatest love. Now he calls us to follow him, trusting that our eternal rewards will far outweigh the temporary struggles.

Once we are able to remove the obstacles to faith produced by the problem of pain and suffering, we are in a much better position to see God more clearly.

## The Heavens Declare the Glory of God

God's power is not relative nor quantitative—it is absolute. What he *can* do knows no bounds; what he *has* done surpasses our ability to understand it. I recently looked at an encyclopedia article about our universe in order to have my mind spin a bit as I contemplated the creative power of God. The article defined a galaxy as a "massive ensemble of hundreds of millions of stars, all gravitationally interacting, and orbiting about a common center. All the stars visible to the unaided eye from earth belong to the earth's galaxy, the Milky Way. The sun with its associated planets is just one star in this galaxy."[4] The article further described the earth's galaxy as one of a small group of about 20 galaxies that astronomers call the Local Group. The earth's galaxy and the Andromeda galaxy are the two largest members, each with a million million stars.[5]

Our own galaxy, the Milky Way, is unbelievably enormous. Consider the following description of it:

> The Milky Way has been determined to be a large spiral galaxy, with several spiral arms coiling around a central bulge about 10,000 light-years thick. The stars in the central bulge are closer together than those in the arms, where more interstellar clouds of dust and gas are found. The diameter of the disk is about 100,000 light-years. It is surrounded by a larger cloud of hydrogen gas, warped and scalloped at its edges,

[4] "Galaxy," Microsoft® *Encarta*. Copyright 1994 Microsoft Corporation. Copyright 1994 Funk & Wagnall's Corporation.

[5] "Galaxy."

and surrounding this in turn is a spheroidal or somewhat flattened halo that contains many separate, globular clusters of stars mainly lying above or below the disk. This halo may be more than twice as wide as the disk itself. In addition, studies of galactic movements suggest that the Milky Way system contains far more matter than is accounted for by the known disk and attendant clusters—up to 2000 billion times more mass than the sun contains.[6]

Are you impressed? Our little galaxy has a million million stars, plus or minus a few. And yet, we live in only one of *thousands* of galaxies. In fact, the largest known galaxy has 13 times as many stars as earth's galaxy. But there is something even more impressive. In 1991, a quasar, (a quasi-stellar object among the most distant and luminous in the universe) was discovered 12 *billion* light-years distant from us. The power of a quasar is astounding. It is said that some of them "produce more energy than 2000 ordinary galaxies—one, S50014 + 81, may be 60,000 times as bright as the Milky Way."[7]

Whose mind can grasp such figures? Billions and billions of stars, trillions of light-years away. One light-year is the distance light travels in one year. At the speed of light (186,000 miles per second), light travels nearly six trillion miles in one year. We are talking about multiplying twelve billion by six trillion to figure the distance in miles from earth to that quasar! Would you even know what to call a number that big, 72 billion trillion?

God made everything in the sky that we have discovered, everything we will ever discover, and everything we will never discover! In the simple affirmations of Scripture, we are informed:

"He determines the number of the stars
    and calls them each by name" (Psalm 147:4).

[6] "Milky Way," Microsoft® *Encarta.* Copyright 1994 Microsoft Corporation. Copyright 1994 Funk & Wagnall's Corporation.
[7] "Quasar," Microsoft® *Encarta.* Copyright 1994 Microsoft Corporation. Copyright 1994 Funk & Wagnall's Corporation.

> "Lift your eyes and look to the heavens:
>     Who created all these?
> He who brings out the starry host one by one,
>     and calls them each by name.
> Because of his great power and mighty strength,
>     not one of them is missing" (Isaiah 40:26).

Volumes have been written about the power of God as seen in all aspects of his creation. Yet, we only see a small amount of creation and understand only a fraction of what we see. Our world is incredibly large and complex; the One who made it resides far beyond our comprehension. Does it not strike you as rather strange that tiny, ignorant, incapable man would question him, and rebel against him, and not trust him? If we could not trust him and his goodness toward us, we would not still be around to even consider such questions. Given who he is and who we are, he undoubtedly is on our side, or we would have been ashes long ago. "I know that you can do all things; no plan of yours can be thwarted" (Job 42:2). "For nothing is impossible with God" (Luke 1:37). Look up; look in; breathe a long sigh of relief; and trust GOD!

## Miracles Are Still Possible

Looking at God's physical creation is impressive. No—staggering! But do you see the possibility of miracles in our day, in your life? To my mind, the greatest of all miracles are seen when God is able to take millions of details in our lives and work them all together for good if we love him (Romans 8:28). For God to exercise his power without the potential interference of others is one thing, but to exercise it with millions of humans often working against him is quite another! He must work through all kinds of people and situations in order to work his purposes out. His power has to be exerted in a way which allows the free choices of men, righteous *and* unrighteous, to remain truly free.

Yet, God's power can overcome all obstacles in the accomplishment of his purposes.

A part of this divine ability comes from the timeless nature of God. He not only sees the end from the beginning—he lives in both at once. Thus, he can arrange the circumstances in order to weave the perfect cloth of his designs into his planned outcome. But how can the free moral agency of man and foreknowledge of God co-exist? If he sees our responses as reality before they occur in time, can we really help doing them? Yes, we are still choosing freely and are still responsible. Because God sees them "ahead of time" does not mean he changes them for us. Yet he remains all-powerful and totally in control of the ultimate outcome.

Consider a large cruise ship. Its final port is selected and the final outcome predetermined. However, as it cruises, all passengers are free to do virtually anything they decide every day. They go to bed when they decide, wake up at the time of their choice, eat what they want, and participate in the recreation they choose. They are totally free within the parameters of the ship's overall policies, but they will arrive at their destination. Similarly, God allows man to make choices, some of which will be good while others will be bad. Yet, he is in control of the final destination, and has both the knowledge and power to accomplish his desired ends.

Tozer's words provide an apt description of how God's knowledge and power work together in wisdom:

> Wisdom, among other things, is the ability to devise perfect ends and to achieve those ends by the most perfect means. It sees the end from the beginning, so there can be no need to guess or conjecture. Wisdom sees everything in focus, each in proper relation to all, and is thus able to work toward predestined goals with flawless precision.
>
> All God's acts are done in perfect wisdom, first for His own glory, and then for the highest good of the greatest number for the longest time. And all His acts are as pure as they are

wise, and as good as they are wise and pure. Not only could
His acts not be better done: a better way to do them could not
be imagined.[8]

## Power with Purpose

Yes, God knows everything and has the power to do
everything he chooses to do. But herein lies our challenge: He
does not choose to do some, or perhaps many, things we ask him
to do. Rather than develop bad attitudes toward him, we need to
understand how his actions are always governed by his purposes.

We have a very finite view of life colored by our tendency to
see things through a physical filter. Although God created the
physical universe, he is focused on the more important spiritual
realm. Therefore, we can expect him to do all that fits into his
plans to develop us spiritually and little that does not promote
this overriding purpose. Unencumbered by a short-term view,
he is unwilling to answer our short-sighted requests. He sees the
eternal perspective and deals with his children accordingly.
Sentimentality is not a part of his nature!

Once I was visiting with a friend who had a young son who
was just beginning to walk. It was obvious that he loved his son
deeply. However, during my visit his son would question that
love. While we adults were talking, the little guy was climbing all
over his dad. At one point, my friend's face turned white in
shock. His son, with some fierceness, had bitten him on the
back. The father had a face-to-face talk with his son and gave him
a serious explanation about why such behavior was unacceptable!

The boy soon returned to his playing and once again climbed
all over his father. After a while, the startled look appeared on
the dad's face again. The "back-biter" had struck once more.
This time Dad did more than explain; he added a little "applied
psychology" to his son's lower extremities. The boy cried as if his

[8] Tozer, pp. 60-61.

heart would break. It seemed to him that his world had turned upside down and his father had lost his love for him. However, the child's view was extremely limited. Even though the father didn't enjoy dishing out such discipline, he wasn't overly affected emotionally. He was much more concerned about the long-term need for discipline and character development in his son than about the boy's immediate pain.

Similarly, God says, "Those whom I love I rebuke and discipline. So be earnest, and repent" (Revelation 3:19). God, from his eternal perspective, uses his perfect knowledge and power to develop righteous character in those he loves. We must decide that we will not question his knowledge, power or goodness. He has no greater concern than blessing our lives spiritually. When we wonder why life seems to be difficult and even unhappy, we need to look past our little world into eternity.

What were you worrying about one year ago today? Can you even remember? We waste far too much time fretting about the temporal and spend too little time remembering our ultimate destiny. Paul saw this issue clearly:

> Therefore we do not lose heart. Though outwardly we are wasting away, yet inwardly we are being renewed day by day. For our light and momentary troubles are achieving for us an eternal glory that far outweighs them all. So we fix our eyes not on what is seen, but on what is unseen. For what is seen is temporary, but what is unseen is eternal (2 Corinthians 4:16-18).

The concerns we have today need to be weighed on the scales of eternity. Just how big will your problems be a year from now? Ten years from now? A hundred years, a thousand years, a million years from now? God looks forward to the future for which he designed us, longing for the close fellowship it holds in store. His knowledge and power will never be used to do anything but bless you. Trust him. Let the words of the beloved apostle clear bless you. Trust him. Let the words of the beloved apostle clear up your view, settle your heart, and thrill your soul:

> And I heard a loud voice from the throne saying, "Now the dwelling of God is with men, and he will live with them. They will be his people, and God himself will be with them and be their God. He will wipe every tear from their eyes. There will be no more death or mourning or crying or pain, for the old order of things has passed away" (Revelation 21:3-4).

# God Desires the Best for Us

Once we understand God's omniscience and omnipotence, we may be more susceptible to faith struggles than ever before. If God *knows* all things and can *do* all things, why does he not protect us from hardships and pain? After all, Jesus did teach us to pray, "And lead us not into temptation, but deliver us from the evil one" (Matthew 6:13). We began our look at these issues in the previous chapter and in this chapter we will examine them thoroughly because our confidence in the love of God is at stake.

## Do You Trust God's Love?

Scripture clearly teaches that everything does come from the hand of God. Consider the following passages:

> "*I form the light and create darkness,*
> *I bring prosperity and create disaster;*
> *I, the LORD, do all these things*" *(Isaiah 45:7).*

> "*Who can speak and have it happen*
> *if the Lord has not decreed it?*
> *Is it not from the mouth of the Most High*
> *that both calamities and good things come?*"
> *(Lamentations 3:37-38).*

Even the very existence of Satan is under God's control and allowed by him. When Satan offered Jesus the kingdoms of the world (Matthew 4:8-9), they were his to offer because God allowed him to have such power. When calamity befell Job, it was definitely at Satan's hand, but God was allowing it to happen to serve his own purposes. As troubling as it may be to us, we have to accept the fact that all evil in the world is at least tolerated by God, although it is not approved by him.

A helpful distinction is made when we differentiate between God's *ideal* will and his *allowed* will. His ideal will is for us to make righteous choices as defined by the Bible. His allowed will results from his decree for man to make his own choices. Since he allows us this freedom, he must tolerate our choices, at least until Judgment Day.

We can sometimes see in Scripture how God's allowed will ties in with his ideal will. The story of Joseph provides a powerful example. In Genesis 50:20 Joseph tells his brothers, "You intended to harm me, but God intended it for good to accomplish what is now being done, the saving of many lives." What his brothers did to Joseph was not God's ideal will. He wills for brothers to love and not harm each other. But the evil they did was included in his allowed will because he intended to use it to accomplish his purposes: the saving of many lives. Thus, even a bad event can be ascribed to the will or actions of God.

At issue in these matters is the overall authority of God. Some things fall into the realm of his ideal will and are directly caused by him. Other things fall into the realm of his tolerated will and are allowed by him. In either case, he is in control of what occurs. Everything which occurs is caused or allowed by him, for he is sovereign over all events. And we must accept the good with thanksgiving and the bad with faith, believing all falls under the umbrella of his mighty will in one way or another. He promised that in *all* things he will work for our good, if we are faithful to him (Romans 8:28).

We must see God's goodness and love working in concert with his knowledge and power. The Bible makes the goodness of God as clear as any subject could possibly be made in writing. He unquestionably desires the very best for each of his creatures.

Since we may be more familiar with NT passages regarding God's desires to bless us in his love, let's look at a few from the OT. As you read them, let your heart drink deeply from the grace and love they offer to us.

> *In your unfailing love you will lead*
> *    the people you have redeemed.*
> *In your strength you will guide them*
> *    to your holy dwelling (Exodus 15:13).*

> *And he passed in front of Moses, proclaiming, "The LORD, the LORD, the compassionate and gracious God, slow to anger, abounding in love and faithfulness, maintaining love to thousands, and forgiving wickedness, rebellion and sin" (Exodus 34:6-7a).*

> *Know therefore that the LORD your God is God; he is the faithful God, keeping his covenant of love to a thousand generations of those who love him and keep his commands (Deuteronomy 7:9).*

> *All the ways of the LORD are loving and faithful*
> *    for those who keep the demands of his covenant*
> *    (Psalm 25:10).*

> *Your love, O LORD, reaches to the heavens,*
> *    your faithfulness to the skies (Psalm 36:5).*

> *You are forgiving and good, O LORD,*
> *    abounding in love to all who call to you (Psalm 86:5).*

> *For great is your love, higher than the heavens;*
> *    your faithfulness reaches to the skies (Psalm 108:4).*

> *"Can a mother forget the baby at her breast*
> *    and have no compassion on the child she has borne?*
> *Though she may forget,*
> *    I will not forget you!" (Isaiah 49:15).*

*"For I know the plans I have for you," declares the* LORD,
*"plans to prosper you and not to harm you, plans to give you*
*hope and a future" (Jeremiah 29:11).*

*"For I take no pleasure in the death of anyone," declares the*
*Sovereign* LORD. *"Repent and live!" (Ezekiel 18:32).*

*"How can I give you up, Ephraim?*
     *How can I hand you over, Israel?...*
*My heart is changed within me;*
     *all my compassion is aroused.*
*I will not carry out my fierce anger,*
     *nor will I turn and devastate Ephraim.*
*For I am God, and not man—*
     *the Holy One among you.*
*I will not come in wrath" (Hosea 11:8-9).*

*"The* LORD *your God is with you,*
     *he is mighty to save.*
*He will take great delight in you,*
     *he will quiet you with his love,*
     *he will rejoice over you with singing" (Zephaniah 3:17).*

If we accepted the testimony of Scripture alone, the fact of
God's love would be unquestionable. However, as humans we
must harmonize our experiences with this testimony.

## What Erodes Trust in God's Love?
*Disappointment with God*

Who among us has never been disappointed with God?
Thankfully, we live in an age when such realities are neither
denied nor sidestepped. It has not always been acceptable to admit
such feelings. In previous generations, to express disappointment
with God or anger toward him was *verboten*.

My grandfather, a minister, died in his early 30s, leaving
behind a young widow and four very small children. My
grandmother chose not to remarry, and faced the very significant

challenge of raising her children alone during the Depression years. I have always suspected that much of who she became as a person was strongly influenced by unexpressed, unresolved anger toward God. Although she was a very religious churchgoer, some of her actions toward her children strongly suggested she had anger locked up inside. When she died in her late 80s, she had been quite ill for months. She seemed to hang on to life tenaciously, as if she were refusing to die. I've always wondered if her difficulty letting go was related to her fear of meeting the God with whom she had been angry without admitting it and working through it.

All of us must figure out how to deal with disappointment with God. The Psalmist provides us with a great example of resolving such inner conflicts with our Maker. Many of the Psalms begin with very strong expressions of disappointment and even anger toward God. But before the end of the Psalm, the writer works through it and feels resolved with God. (The only exception I can remember is Psalm 88, in which he closes with the sad comment that the darkness was his closest friend! I assume he wrote another Psalm of resolution quickly.)

How does God feel when we express disappointment or anger? If you are a parent, how do you feel when your children express such attitudes toward you? I'm always ready to hear it and anxious to help them work through their hurts. The only restriction I place on such conversations is that respect is maintained. Other than this, I welcome such interactions. It surely beats them carrying such feelings around in their hearts without expressing their hurts and resolving them. If I can accept such honesty, and even encourage it, surely the greatest possible Father has no problem with helping his children work through their emotional pains.

A word of caution is in order. When man's negative attitudes toward God move from emotional pain to long-standing intellectual arguments, he has crossed the line. Job eventually crossed this line, and God called him to account in no uncertain terms. But for many days, God allowed Job to express much disappointment and emotional pain. However, when he began marshaling his case intellectually, even stating a desire to face God in a court of justice, he had gone past the point of emotionality and into sin.

A similar account is seen in Romans 9, where the people were making arguments against the justice of God. In this case, Paul wrote,

> One of you will say to me: "Then why does God still blame us? For who resists his will?" But who are you, O man, to talk back to God? "Shall what is formed say to him who formed it, 'Why did you make me like this?'" (Romans 9:19-20).

All of us will struggle at some point in our attempt to harmonize the power of God with his refusal to intervene and protect us from pain. We will feel disappointment, and likely anger. To feel such is not sin, if we verbalize it and work it through. Any decent father is willing and eager to help his children work through similar difficulties in their relationship with him. No close relationship can exist for long without misunderstandings, hurts and disappointments. Therefore, we must learn to resolve them quickly and thoroughly, whether with family, friends or God. This issue of being disappointed with God is a serious one. It may not seem large to many people, only because it is so difficult to admit being mad at an all-knowing, all-powerful, all-loving Being. Such feelings seem ludicrous (and they are), but they are *real* and must be reckoned with even though we know intellectually that he is always right and we are always wrong at these times. Let's get real, get honest, and deal with the realities of human responses to difficult times. I am not defending wrong feelings toward God in the least, but I am dealing with the realities of the human psyche. You and I are hardly more spiritual than the Psalmist, so don't let self-righteousness get the better of you!

One of the best books I have read on this subject is *Disappointment With God* by Philip Yancey.[1] Appropriately, the sub-title is *Three Questions No One Asks Aloud*. These questions are: "Is God Unfair?" "Is God Silent?" and "Is God Hidden?" These questions are right on target, addressing the way we humans are tempted to reason. But when we examine them carefully, the truth shows the futility of worrying about the answers.

To question one, "Is God Unfair?" we should begin by realizing that if God were simply fair, all of us would be in hell already! We only *think* we want fairness from him! (*We actually want grace!*) And if we expect life to be fair, we are living in a dream world. Sinners inhabit this planet, and you and I are among them. Those of us with the greatest intentions are sometimes guilty of being unfair to those closest to us. And most people around us do not have the greatest intentions. Life was never fair to Jesus Christ, the world's only sinless man. Why should we expect more than he received? Those who get incensed easily about unfairness are destined for a life of frustration. Be hard on yourself about your own fair treatment of others, but do not rely on it in return. Faith shines brightest when the circumstances militate against it.

The question of God's silence comes from the type of heart Job had when he was in sin. We want God to speak up in some way and explain why his world is hurting us. But he is not in the explaining business. He is God, and that is all he needs to be. He owes no one an explanation. Thankfully, he chose to explain all we need to know in the Bible. A righteous life is based on the continual choice to walk by faith and not by sight (2 Corinthians 5:7). Hanging on to God when it doesn't make sense to the worldly-minded is to honor and please God immeasurably. To continue questioning him beyond the emotional reaction stage is to dishonor him and displease him.

[1] Philip Yancey, *Disappointment With God* (Harper Paperbacks, a Division of Harper Collins Publishers, 1991 edition).

The third question, "Is God Hidden?" relates to the second one. As physical beings, we have trouble trusting what we cannot actually see. We long for God to show himself, at least by giving us some tangible signs. Even though he did such for Gideon and others in the Bible, these signs were certainly the exception to the rule. We must walk by faith and not by sight. If we insist on God giving us "signs," we are setting ourselves up for disappointment at best, and receiving signs from Satan at worst! (2 Thessalonians 2:9-12).

Yancy goes back to the wilderness wandering period of the Israelites to help us to answer these three questions. God was fair. He made some amazing promises about people not getting sick, women not miscarrying, and shoes not wearing out. But the promises were predicated on the obedience of the people. They fell in the wilderness by the thousands as the plagues for disobedience were fairly applied! He was neither silent nor hidden. He showed himself in the pillars of fire and cloud and in the storms at Mount Sinai. He spoke aloud and shook the mountain. How happy were the people with this behavior of God? They pleaded for him to appear only to Moses and speak only to him.

At a time when God was so obvious, God's people were never less faithful. What we mistakenly long for is absolutely opposite of faith. We may honestly struggle with disappointment with God, but eventually we must see whose problem it is! Be honest about negative feelings toward God, and work through them. But do it humbly and quickly, and at such times be open to seeing that you are the one with the wrong perspective. God is God. He cannot be wrong nor can he be unloving. Trust him and persevere through the faith-testing times. Nothing shows our love for God more clearly. Keep on keeping on and you will encourage God!

### Disillusionment Through Failure

I literally *hate* failure. How about you? Surely some of my disdain of failure comes from good motives, a desire to please

God and serve others effectively. But some (maybe *much*, or even *most*) of my feelings come from my prideful desires to be successful and to appear impressive. We have to learn how to define success and failure.

However you may choose to define these terms, the definition must be a long-range one. Some people are very impressive in their accomplishments in the short-term and abject failures over the long haul. They, like shooting stars, spread a bright light and then disappear into the darkness. All of us who claim to be disciples want to make things happen for Jesus. We want to lead others to Christ and to help form him in their lives. These are biblical desires, and we are called to become the best we can be for him.

But you will have to learn to deal with failures. And you will have to learn to be humble. If failures only awaken your pride and make you more determined than ever not to fail again, you can look forward to some huge challenges in your future. God will not take his hand off of you until you become humble. You can pull yourself up by your own bootstraps just so many times. Failures are designed to make you rely on God. Claiming reliance on God or preaching it does not mean you are God-reliant. We all learn the right things to say. Terminology is not the issue—heart is.

For the most part, true success in serving God is ultimately measured in perseverance. Failure in serving God comes when we give up and quit the battle, either outwardly or inwardly. You may keep going through the spiritual motions for years, but when you lose faith and give up inside your heart of hearts, you have failed. At this point, you will either wake up and repent, or you will proceed down the deceptive path of lukewarmness and deadness until you are no longer recognizable as a disciple. Maintaining faith is the clarion call for our lives, year-in and year-out, in good times and bad, whether short-term success or failure comes our way.

The impact of our lives can never be seen before eternity reveals it to us. But rest assured that a life of devotion and faith cannot fail. Time will yield its rewards to those who abide in Christ (John 15:1-8). Do not let Satan use one of his most effective tools on you—*discouragement*. In Galatians 6:9 Paul gives us a challenge and a promise: "Let us not become weary in doing good, for at the proper time we will reap a harvest if we do not give up." Our victories are predicated on keeping faith. "This is the victory that has overcome the world, even our faith" (1 John 5:4).

## How Can We Restore Trust in God's Love?
*A Return to Idealism*

In Matthew 18:3, Jesus made this rather shocking statement: "I tell you the truth, unless you change and become like little children, you will never enter the kingdom of heaven." We have many lessons to learn from children, and if we are to enter heaven, we must learn them. The preceding section defined faith in terms of perseverance, which is an essential ingredient in faith, but the perseverance must have a certain childlike quality about it.

Although faith certainly has nothing to do with pessimism, it is more than optimism. Faith is better described as "spiritual idealism." From children we can learn about idealism. They remain idealistic in the face of all kinds of disappointments, at least during their early childhood years. Their responses to questions demonstrate the point. "What are you going to be when you grow up, son?" "A fireman and an astronaut!" When their family setting is terrible, they find a way to look at the positive side and avoid the worst conclusions. God made them in such a way that they cannot bear the burdens of admitting that their mother is a prostitute and their father a drunk. They will find a way to maintain idealism and look at the brightest side possible.

In Chapter One I referred to Fantine's line from *Les Miserables*: "Life has killed the dream I dreamed." Many people can relate to these words. Life beats the idealism out of children at some point, and as spiritual children, we can allow life to have the same impact on us. The challenge of Jesus is to avoid the loss of idealism, viewing such a loss as great tragedy. But what is an idealistic faith?

*Idealistic faith is a faith untarnished by the passage of time.* Joseph clung to his idealism for 13 long years and was rewarded by the God who never fails. Caleb set his sights on a certain mountain when he was 40 years old and never gave up his dream until he received it 45 years later. He refused to let his dream die, even as he attended funerals by the thousands as the rest of his generation, arguably the most faithless in the history of Israel, died in the wilderness. Like a kid, he said in his advanced years, "I am still as strong today as the day Moses sent me out; I'm just as vigorous to go out to battle now as I was then. Now give me this hill country that the LORD promised me that day" (Joshua 14:11-12).

*Idealistic faith in a right sense is "not confused by the facts."* The greatest fact is God; all other facts cannot dim our view of him. The father of the faithful, Abraham, *faced* the fact that his body was as good as dead (Romans 4:19), and then *faithed* the facts! Facts are no longer impressive nor persuasive when God enters the picture. Joshua led his men into battle after an all-night march and longed for more daylight in which to continue the battle. Then amazingly, he prayed in the sight of all his men for the sun to stand still. I could understand praying an outlandish prayer in private, but this fellow blurted it out in public! Facts, even scientific ones, apparently didn't mean much to him. And as it turned out, they didn't mean much to the God who designed them:

> *The sun stopped in the middle of the sky and delayed going down about a full day. There has never been a day like it before or since, a day when the LORD listened to a man. Surely the LORD was fighting for Israel! (Joshua 10:13-14).*

We are prone to look at the facts of what has or has not been done, and reach our conclusions accordingly. So what if it has never been done before? Maybe it's time to do it for the first time in the name of God.

*Idealistic faith is not halted by fears.* Paul may have come into the city of Corinth "in weakness and fear, and with much trembling" (1 Corinthians 2:3), but he did not back down or bow out. He stayed for 18 months and established a great church. Later, in encouraging Timothy to follow his example, he wrote, "For God did not give us a spirit of timidity, but a spirit of power, of love and of self-discipline" (2 Timothy 1:7). If the spirit of timidity does not come from God, it doesn't take long to figure out from whence it comes! Comfort zones would better be called "danger zones" or even "death zones." The roll call of hell begins with the *cowardly* (Revelation 21:8). Fighter pilots are almost always young men, because they still have the spirit of reckless abandon. Fighters for God, regardless of age, must be young at heart and full of the same spirit of adventure which refuses to bow the knee to fear.

*The faith of idealism is not destroyed by failures.* The amazing thing about God is that he always has a Plan B for us. Actually, because of our failures to live up to his Plan A for us, we are perhaps on Plan ZZZ. But no matter—God has promised to work all things together for our good. Just what Plan A for my life might have been is almost scary to contemplate. However, through my sin and weakness, I destroyed that plan years ago. God keeps on working to move us in the direction of the best plan available at every juncture of our lives. Never give up on yourself, because the God who longs to orchestrate the days of your life has not given up on you. Keep your idealism and keep moving forward. The God of all grace stands ready to direct your steps!

## The Excitement of Grace

The grace of God provides the most effective renewal of trust in God possible. I spent years in a denomination not known for an emphasis on grace, but I can remember a few key sermons which thrilled my soul nearly beyond belief. Some of the illustrations will remain in my heart for time and eternity. The concept of "walking in the light," according to 1 John 1:5-10, was one which was explained with effective illustrations. The verb "purifies" here denotes a continual action. Just as windshield wipers continually wipe away the water, the blood of Christ continually takes away our sins and keeps us saved. As blood in our physical body continually removes impurities from our system, Christ's blood constantly removes impurities from those in his spiritual body (the church).[2]

Walking in the light suggests a faithful and consistent walk with God. The unrighteous person follows Satan consistently and will end up with him, even though he occasionally turns aside from that path and does *good* things. The righteous person follows Christ consistently and will end up with him, even though he occasionally turns aside from that path and does *bad* things. The real issue is faithfulness—the heart and the overall issue of one's life. None of us is *perfect*, but any of us can be *faithful*. The difference between faithfulness and perfection can be illustrated by asking my wife if I am a *perfect* husband (definitely "No"). On the other hand, if asked whether I am a *faithful* husband, she would say definitely "Yes"!

One of my favorite biblical terms is *justified*. The original Greek word was used in legal settings to signify *innocent* or *not guilty*. In a practical sense, we can say it means "just-as-if-I'd" never sinned!" Once I was working on a message for a teen audience about the need to make choices for God at a young age.

[2] "Walking in the light" *cannot* mean perfection or sinlessness. Otherwise, there would be no sins of which to be cleansed (verse 7).

I was thinking about my own teen years. I had made many wrong choices that I later regretted. I thought back about the influence I might have had on my schoolmates if I had made godly choices and wished that I could go back and exert this spiritual influence on my friends of long ago.

As I then thought about the term *justified*, it occurred to me that even if I had lived 100 times better than I did live, complete with a positive influence on others, I could not be any more right with God! To be viewed by God *just-as-if-I'd never sinned* is as good as it can be! (Obviously, to have made spiritual choices earlier would have benefited many others, and myself as well—sin leaves its consequences emotionally even on forgiven people.) But today my *standing* with God is absolutely right—*perfect* in the blood of the Lamb! This sounds too good to be true, doesn't it? It *is* indescribably good, but altogether true. Understanding these precious truths should change our way of looking at God and at our lives for him in a *radical* manner!

Because of the astounding grace and love of God, you can live with no sin ever being credited to your account (Romans 4:8). He wants you to see yourself the way he sees you and to realize your inestimable value as a creation of his. But many Christians struggle with continued feelings of worthlessness because they know all too well what they were like before becoming Christians, and they are quite aware of their sins as Christians. However, their problem is that they neither understand grace nor that their own value is based on their nature rather than their performance. Let the following little illustration find its way to your heart:

An ugly bilious green chair sat on top of a trash pile awaiting the arrival of the garbage truck. Those who passed by and saw the chair thought to themselves, "I don't blame those people for throwing that hideous chair away. In fact, I wonder why they ever kept it to begin with?"

However, one person had an entirely different reaction when he passed by and saw the chair. He quickly pulled his station wagon over to the curb, jumped out and grabbed the chair, put it in the back of his vehicle and drove away. When this antique dealer got the chair home, he began stripping off the many coats of paint until he was down to the original wood. Once restored, this chair was a thing of beauty and value! To the eyes of the unaware, the chair was junk, but to the trained eye of the antique dealer, it was an object to be esteemed. The layers of ugly paint did not take away the basic nature of the chair underneath it all.

Similarly, we have "painted" up our own lives with many ugly coats of sin, but the real value remains underneath the surface. Once these hideous layers are removed by the blood of Christ, our true nature may be seen once more. But what is it about our nature that gives us value in the first place? It is that we are made in the image of God himself (Genesis 1:27). We have the capability to reason, to feel, to appreciate, to love. And we have the capacity to live for eternity!

But how can we be sure that we are really valuable after all? Our value has been permanently established by the price God paid for us: his becoming a man and dying on the cross in our place. For a shirt, we might be willing to pay $20 or $30 and maybe more (depending on our financial situation and the quality of the shirt). But no one would pay $1,000,000 for it. The price we are willing to pay for something reflects its value to us. When God paid this unbelievable price for our souls, he set our value far beyond man's ability to comprehend it. Let's believe that and then let's live like we believe it! Get excited about the grace of God, and see him and yourself as who both of you really are. We were created in the image of God and redeemed by the blood of his Son.

## Conclusion

The biblical demands, examples and rewards are all part of what motivates us to change. However, we will never plunge into the exciting waters of surrender and remain there until and unless we gain the right view of God.

When we see God as he has revealed himself, surrender is the only course which makes sense at all. He knows all, can do all, and desires to only do those things which will ultimately lead us to heaven. Finally, consider these insightful words of Tozer as he describes the love of God:

> His love is measureless. It is more: it is boundless. It has no bounds because it is not a thing but a facet of the essential nature of God. His love is something He is, and because He is infinite that love can enfold the whole created world in itself and have room for ten thousand times ten thousand worlds besides....
>
> It is a strange and beautiful eccentricity of the free God that He has allowed His heart to be emotionally identified with men. Self-sufficient as He is, He wants our love and will not be satisfied till He gets it. Free as He is, He has let His heart be bound to us forever.[3]

[3] Tozer, pp. 47, 100.

# Epilogue

In this book, I have attempted to provide a biblical treatment of the element of faith sometimes called "surrender." My study of surrender has been one of the most enlightening of my life, and I pray that the material presented here has helped you to understand your faith response to the God who loves you dearly. While I certainly don't know everything about this subject (or any other!), I do know some things about it.

## Some Things I Know

I know that surrender is the most fundamental aspect of faith in God, for it allows him to *be* God in our lives. I know that an understanding of the inherent principles in surrender explains much about the events that come our way. Even when such understanding is hindsight, it is comforting to see why God allowed into my life the things which may have been challenging or confusing initially. I also know that surrender in practice is always challenging, but extremely rewarding. At times in life I may struggle with surrender, but the peace it brings to my heart thrills me to the depths of my being.

I remember an instance which occurred during my early study of the subject. I was praying urgently for a specific blessing from God and ended up in the "If you will, I will…" mode. But then I started thinking through what I would give up to God if he would answer the prayer. I couldn't think of one thing which was not already laid on the altar to God. I had already surrendered my possessions, my family, my health, my future, my life and death, and anything else I could think about surrendering. As it dawned on me how surrendered I felt at that moment, my soul felt as if it was going to soar out of my body. To have a relationship with God in which absolutely nothing is consciously held back is exhilarating beyond description. Surrender works wonders in the human heart and life. Of this truth I am absolutely sure.

## Some Things I May Never Know

On the other hand, understanding the principles of surrender does not clear up all mysteries. Two situations in my life illustrate that we will not always understand how God is working. In the first, I was contemplating a move to another part of the country to minister for a certain congregation in my former denomination. Although another man was also being considered, I was confident that they were going to offer me the job. To my dismay, the other man received the position, and I was left licking my wounded ego. For a long time, I wondered why God had seemingly led me in a direction only to disappoint me. However, I was later fortunate enough to be given further insight into the nature of that church so that I was able to actually rejoice that I was not hired by them. God spared me a lot of grief. In this case, my initial confusion was followed by a time of understanding and gratitude.

But sometimes we never figure out why he allows some events in our lives. Several years after being rejected by the church just mentioned, I accepted a position with another church in the same part of the country. In the former case, God said "No" and in the latter case, he said "Yes." (However, I often wished he had said "No" both times!)

Although I enjoyed that ministry in many ways, the impact on my family was not positive. Some in the congregation were small thinkers and thus negative thinkers. Since I was reasonably unflappable, the negative folks turned their criticism toward my family, even though my children were very young at the time. Suffice it to say that harm was done at a level we had never experienced in that fellowship of churches up to that time. By the grace of God, my children are doing great with the Lord today, but we all bear some scars from that experience. Why did God allow us to move there and undergo the pains? Frankly, I do not know. I have thought and prayed about it a good deal, but I am not at all sure what God intended to accomplish in the situation.

In an early chapter, I mentioned that my grandfather, a minister, had died when quite young and left a young widow with four small children to raise through the Depression years. Why did God allow it? I don't have a clue. I can imagine some scenarios in which his death might have worked into an overall plan which ended up blessing my life, but it is pure speculation. Surrender does not give me insight into all that happens in my life. It does give me the faith and determination to hold on to God even tighter when problems come instead of tempting me to leave him. But some things I may never know. As Paul phrased it in 2 Corinthians 5:7, "We live by faith, not by sight."

## One Thing I Must Know

Life with God is much like a roller coaster ride. It is filled with ups and downs, exhilaration and terror, but it is never boring. In the midst of the variety of experiences and challenges we all face, how do we keep our bearings? Paul distilled his life with God into a simple formula, according to Philippians 3:13-14:

*Brothers, I do not consider myself yet to have taken hold of it. But one thing I do: Forgetting what is behind and straining toward what is ahead, I press on toward the goal to win the prize for which God has called me heavenward in Christ Jesus.*

In the broader context, Paul's secret of remaining surrendered could be described in terms of *losing* and *gaining*. Philippians 3:7-8 tells us that Paul suffered the loss of all things which had been precious to him. He had quite a background as a Jew but was willing to sacrifice it for the sake of Christ. He viewed his accomplishments and material advantages as mere rubbish when compared to the value of knowing and serving Jesus. Therefore, once Paul had freed himself from the burdens of the physical realm, the "one thing" he was concentrating on was his (and others') spiritual growth. I will never be happy unless I am willing to give up anything and everything for the sake of God's kingdom. Nor will you.

Paul, in Philippians 3:9-11, next described what he longed to gain. Note the nature of his singular focus:

> *I want to know Christ and the power of his resurrection and the fellowship of sharing in his sufferings, becoming like him in his death (Philippians 3:10).*

Paul was not satisfied with knowing *about* Jesus. Nor was he content with having a casual relationship with him. He wanted to become like his Lord in suffering and in dying. His surrender was complete. The glitter of this world no longer held any enticements for him, nor did its threats affect his security in the least. He was relaxed and confident; contented and serene; willing to live or willing to die. I have realized that if I am to have that same spirit and outlook, I must say with Paul, "There is one thing I must know. *I must know Christ*, the power of his resurrection and the fellowship of sharing in his suffering."

The surrendered disciple will find the power to face life's roughest moments with the outlook expressed by a surrendered prophet:

> *Though the fig tree does not bud*
> *    and there are no grapes on the vines,*
> *though the olive crop fails*

> *and the fields produce no food,*
> *though there are no sheep in the pen*
>     *and no cattle in the stalls,*
> *yet I will rejoice in the LORD,*
>     *I will be joyful in God my Savior"* *(Habakkuk 3:17-18).*

The surrendered disciple will also find the power to face life's end with the confidence expressed by a surrendered apostle:

> *If we live, we live to the Lord; and if we die, we die to the Lord. So, whether we live or die, we belong to the Lord.*
>
> *For this very reason, Christ died and returned to life so that he might be the Lord of both the dead and the living (Romans 14:8-9).*
>
> *Who shall separate us from the love of Christ? Shall trouble or hardship or persecution or famine or nakedness or danger or sword? As it is written:*
>
> *"For your sake we face death all day long;*
>     *we are considered as sheep to be slaughtered."*
>
> *No, in all these things we are more than conquerors through him who loved us. For I am convinced that neither death nor life, neither angels nor demons, neither the present nor the future, nor any powers, neither height nor depth, nor anything else in all creation, will be able to separate us from the love of God that is in Christ Jesus our Lord (Romans 8:35-39).*

With such faith let us live, and with such faith let us die. Since all the days ordained for you and me were written in God's book before one of them came to be (Psalm 139:16), to do less than surrender is nothing short of insanity. In our right minds, let us face God, ourselves and life's ultimate destiny. *The victory of surrender* will then be ours for time and for eternity. *Amen! Hallelujah! And to God be the glory!*

# Appendix

# Surrender and Finding the Will of God

Discovering the will of God for our lives seems at times to be an elusive goal. How can we determine which decisions are in keeping with God's plan for us? Much of what has been said about this topic is riddled with subjectivity and likely to mislead. The seeking of "signs" and "inner promptings" of the Holy Spirit often leads us in the opposite direction of true surrender, thus allowing "self" to reign supreme.

However, the Bible does talk about finding and following the will of God. Most of the biblical references to the will of God are simply describing (1) his sovereign plan for the world or (2) his moral will for our lives as expressed in his Word. Knowledge in either of these realms comes only through what he has revealed. Other references appear to refer to a third element: his will (or plan) for our individual lives. He does have such a plan, although we may discover it through hindsight rather than foresight!

As each of us seeks God's will for our personal lives, we need to keep a few practical principles in mind in order to avoid confusion. One, many of our everyday decisions are not highly significant in their importance. In such instances, God is quite willing for us to make any one of several choices. Two, such decisions usually are not issues of right and wrong, but rather good, better and best. Three, when our choices are more significant, the outcome of the decisions themselves are not the only factor to consider. Our personal character development should also be taken into consideration. Developing a spiritual mindset is just as important as making the "right" decision.

In the first two categories, we should always be spiritually-minded and kingdom-focused without being overly concerned about making mistakes. To worry about "missing the will of God" is fruitless. However, when the decisions are more significant in their impact on us and others, we should be much more deliberate and prayerful (but still never worried). If we are concerned enough to make our decisions in a righteous manner, God will surely lead us in making them. Philippians 3:15-16 contains a very important lesson in this regard. In essence, this passage teaches that if we are not mature enough to grasp God's will at a given point, we should continue to live up to the light we already see, while trusting God to reveal additional light as we go. It is, therefore, a question of *process* and *progress*. God often leads us within the process of trial and error. But if we remain faithful and surrendered through even the errors, he will lead us onto the path of progress of a greater understanding of his will for us.

But what does surrender have to do with finding the will of God? Simply stated, we cannot see clearly without it. Jesus said,

> *"The eye is the lamp of the body. If your eyes are good, your whole body will be full of light. But if your eyes are bad, your whole body will be full of darkness. If then the light within you is darkness, how great is that darkness!" (Matthew 6:22-23).*

In context, Jesus is warning against having our eyes focused on the physical aspects of life. When we are looking at the world with a materialistic (or humanistic) view, we cannot see God or his will for our lives. When we look at it with a heart surrendered to God's purposes, God is free to make his will evident to us.

As we search the Scriptures for God's will for our individual lives, we must understand at least three qualities inherent in a surrendered heart: humility, commitment and gratitude.

## Humility

> *Now listen, you who say, "Today or tomorrow we will go to this or that city, spend a year there, carry on business and make money." Why, you do not even know what will happen*

*tomorrow. What is your life? You are a mist that appears for*
*a little while and then vanishes. Instead, you ought to say, "If*
*it is the Lord's will, we will live and do this or that." As it is,*
*you boast and brag. All such boasting is evil (James 4:13-16).*

Pride causes one to be a *control freak*, a seeker of his own will
and a boaster in what he intends to accomplish. Since God exalts
the humble and resists the proud, such a person can be sure of
the fall his pride will cause. As the text indicates, keeping a healthy
perspective of one's mortality is necessary for maintaining a
surrendered heart. No matter how long you may live, the end
will come soon enough. The works of your hands soon will be
reduced to a dim memory in the minds of the few who knew you
during your brief sojourn on this earth. Therefore, in view of
eternity, seeking God's way rather than your own is the only
sane policy.

Considering decisions with a heart that says, "If it is the
Lord's will..." provides a remedy for pride. But a word of caution
is in order: Perfunctory repetitions of this phrase will only add
to our problems, as we perhaps fool ourselves and others around
us. God, however, will not be fooled. The issue is not to *sound*
spiritual in decision-making; it is to *be* spiritually surrendered to
the will of God, whatever that will may turn out to be. Are you
willing to make decisions about what job you will take and where
you will live with humility? Are you willing to go against the
grain of your natural tendencies in these areas?

When I made the decision to leave San Diego and move to
Boston in the middle of winter, I was not making an easy decision.
Instead of speaking to a Sunday audience of 1250, I spoke to one
of 50 (and I didn't always have the opportunity to speak to them).
We moved from a beautiful four-bedroom, three-bathroom house
to a two-bedroom apartment. We exchanged the mild breezes of
southern California for the wintry blast of New England. Why?
Because we believed it to be the will of God. We went against the

grain of our natural inclinations, and we did it with humility. The humility was seen in our willingness to take the advice of spiritual leaders whose lives had made far more impact on the world than ours. We needed to listen and learn, surrender and submit, move and be trained. As mentioned earlier in the book, the move turned out to be far better for us than we could have asked or imagined.

As a leader in a very large church, I sometimes hear of members contemplating a decision to move to another city. Often, when the rationalizations are removed, the reasons given are shown not to be spiritual. Moves based on selfish motives weaken our moral fiber. Moves based on kingdom reasons, which always demand the element of self-denial instead of self-gratification, strengthen our spiritual character. In looking at my own life, it is amazing how making the most difficult decisions has yielded the most precious blessings, while making the comfortable, non-threatening decisions has led to few blessings. Surrender demands a willingness to pay any price God asks.

If you are not willing to literally move anywhere, do anything and give up everything for God, you are not wanting to find his will. And you will not find it. God blesses humility. When we draw lines in our lives, refusing to lay certain things on the altar of sacrifice, we will ultimately pay a price. Either we will suffer for our lack of surrender, or we will miss out on what might have been.

The seeking and accepting of spiritual advice is a key factor in determining our level of humility. Without this element, selfishness and pride will have a bigger say in the directions we follow than we might imagine.

As I was writing this section, I contemplated a choice of how to spend my evening. I wanted to do one thing, but felt I should do another. Thus, I called a mature brother who had a grasp of both choices and asked for advice. He gave the advice I didn't want to hear but suspected was correct. I followed it, and during the course of the night, my wife whispered in my ear, "Aren't you glad we followed the advice?" Yes, I was glad, for the will of God had become clear. However, without the determination to ask and heed advice, I would have gone *my* way and missed out on a great experience that allowed me to bless others and to be blessed in the process. Humble out and allow God to direct your steps.

## Commitment

> *Therefore, I urge you, brothers, in view of God's mercy, to offer your bodies as living sacrifices, holy and pleasing to God—this is your spiritual act of worship. Do not conform any longer to the pattern of this world, but be transformed by the renewing of your mind. Then you will be able to test and approve what God's will is—his good, pleasing and perfect will (Romans 12:1-2).*

This passage teaches three fundamental truths regarding the will of God for our lives. One, he has such a will, and it is both pleasing and perfect. It is not simply acceptable or even good; it is best. Two, this will is often discerned through testing. This suggests that it often goes in the opposite direction of our human nature. Three, it can be known by us. The Greek word translated "approve" means "have a certain knowledge of." However, the earlier part of the text gives some *prerequisites* for knowing his will.

The first thing Paul calls us to do is to offer our bodies as living sacrifices to God. He reminds us that such a total commitment must be based on our appreciation of his mercy, for only then will we be able to offer ourselves without reservation or restriction. With the phrase "living sacrifice" Paul is surely wanting to contrast the sacrifice that the disciple of Jesus makes with that made by the people under the Old Covenant. Living sacrifices differ in several basic ways from the animal sacrifices of that first covenant, but the chief difference concerns the idea of limitations.

The animal sacrifices were limited in monetary cost. Even if an animal were expensive for an individual or family, it could be paid for and done with. Not so with a living sacrifice. These are limitless in price, for the debt of love to God can never be paid in full. We are always debtors to the crucified Christ! No payment is ever enough, and none can be made out of simple obligation. All actions of true Christians are ever to be gifts of gratitude for God's unspeakable Gift.

The animal sacrifices also were limited in time costs. A worshipper spent the necessary time to follow God's instructions, and after the sacrifice was over he could go on his way singing "mission accomplished." However, a spiritual sacrifice is never finished until life ends. It is a 24-hour-per-day, seven-days-per-week affair and will never be less. Our time is God's time, and our task his task. As a disciple, I can never sink back into selfishness and say "Now it's my time to do what I want." (Obviously, all of us need to change pace and rest up on occasion, but even in the midst of such times, we are still on the mission of our Redeemer.)

The animal sacrifices were restricted in the location where they could be offered. On the other hand, the location of spiritual offerings is not in any way restricted. Worship is not limited to special buildings or to special times. When I was a young minister, I recall people saying in a Sunday assembly that "We come together to worship." The statement sounds noble enough, doesn't it? However, this can be theologically incorrect. If we only worship when we come together in a religious assembly, we are missing the heart and spirit of Romans 12. A biblically accurate statement regarding assemblies would be "We come to worship *together*," implying that we all worship individually at other times and in other places. But, this truth in no way lessens the need and importance of assembled worship, for the Scripture declares this corporate worship to be vital (Hebrews 10:23-25).

Another prerequisite for being in position to test and approve God's will is non-conformity—we are not to conform to this world. The Phillips translation renders Romans 12:2, "Don't let the world around you squeeze you into its own mold...." Recently I was trying to help a young woman come to some spiritual convictions and decisions about her life. She was lamenting the fact that she had a strong-willed, rebellious spirit. I assured her that either quality could be turned in a right direction. To be like Jesus, we must have strong wills set with godly determination. Otherwise, we will never stay the spiritual course with him. We must also "rebel" against the unrighteous *status quo* all around us, for Jesus certainly did. Disciples, although not rebellious in the normal sense of the term (with arrogance), must stand against the godlessness of the world. The key is to allow God to direct all of our qualities into spiritual channels rather than having them conformed to the world's mold. Just remember that Satan is always trying to distort otherwise good things into evil ones.

The last prerequisite in the passage is that we must undergo a transformation. The word "transformed" comes from the Greek word from which we get our word "metamorphosis." In practical terms, God is not simply asking us to make a few incidental changes; he is asking us to change fundamentally. We are to go from the caterpillar stage of living to the butterfly stage. We put off the worldly attitudes, values and practices, and through the power of the Holy Spirit, put on the godly qualities found in Jesus Christ. This is a continuing process—every disciple must be in process, not sitting still!

Now, once we are following the principles in Romans 12:1-2, we are then in position to be able to determine God's will for our lives. The following context shows that the will being discussed has to do with our own *niche* in God's kingdom. Who of us is not interested in finding our God-given, God-intended roles? Therefore, it is clear that discovering his will for our lives is based on the surrender of our lives to him and to others in his spiritual body, the church. As verse 5 says, "each member belongs to all the others." This surrender is described in terms of offering our bodies as living sacrifices; non-conformity to the world's mold; and transformation of our characters by the renewal of our minds in response to his Word.

Do you want to know what God's will is for your life? You can! But not without a total commitment to the spiritual life described by Paul in Romans 12. Surrender includes humility and commitment, and as we will see in the following section, it must be crowned by a continually thankful heart.

### Gratitude

*Be joyful always; pray continually; give thanks in all circumstances, for this is God's will for you in Christ Jesus (1 Thessalonians 5:16-18).*

We know for sure that God's will for our lives is to rejoice always and to give thanks in all circumstances. Unless we are unwilling to practice this truth, we should expect to discover his individualized will. Finding out just how to accomplish this command is the challenge. As with all worthwhile spiritual endeavors, the way of the cross is the way to accomplish all aspects of the will of God. Without surrender, we can never be sure we have found such a will, and without it, we will never be recipients of the peace that surpasses comprehension.

God's will is not only for us to be surrendered outwardly; it is for us to remain joyful and thankful no matter what the circumstances. In this quality, we must be like Jesus. How would you describe him? If you were to make a list of his qualities, would you include *joyful*? Frankly, too few of us would think of him as a joy-filled person. Humble and committed, for sure; prayerful and thankful, without doubt; but more sober and somber than joyful. Why do we not see Jesus as he really was in this important area?

Our main difficulty is our tendency to confuse happiness with joy. Our idea of happiness is often borrowed from the world, in that it depends too much on outward circumstances. To be happy is to be free from any pressing problem, right? No, for the Christian will never be free from problems and challenges. In fact, by virtue of being followers of Jesus, we have volunteered for constant challenges. He said in John 16:33, "In this world you will have trouble." Thankfully, he preceded this statement with "...in me you may have peace."

In Philippians 4:4, Paul told us to rejoice always, but he modified the command with the phrase "in the Lord." Note the contrast between life in the world and life in Christ. If we depend on the physical aspects of life for joy, we are in for a rough ride. If we depend on our relationship with God, we can remain in a rejoicing state. But even our spiritual activities and accomplishments are not to be the key source of our joy. Jesus said, "However, do not rejoice that the spirits submit to you, but rejoice that your names are written in heaven" (Luke 10:20). Spiritual focus is everything, isn't it?

When Paul and Silas were in a Philippian jail, after having been falsely accused and beaten severely, they prayed and sang hymns (Acts 16:23-25). What would you have done had you been in their place? Frankly, many of us would have been angry at our accusers and disappointed in God. We might wonder if it "paid" to be a follower of Christ. Peter and John earlier suffered similarly, and reacted similarly: "They called the apostles in and had them flogged. Then they ordered them not to speak in the name of Jesus, and let them go. The apostles left the Sanhedrin, rejoicing because they had been counted worthy of suffering disgrace for the Name" (Acts 5:40-41). Only surrendered people can be joyful in such circumstances.

No wonder Paul followed his admonition to "be joyful always" with "pray continually" (1 Thessalonians 5:16-17)! The only way to remain joyful is to pray constantly. But notice in verse 18 of the passage that Paul included thanksgiving as a vital part of this continual prayer mode. He said to be thankful *in* all circumstances (not *for* all circumstances). Some circumstances are not at all good, but God will work good out of them (Romans 8:28). The surrendered disciple of Jesus trusts God to control his life in a manner that brings ultimate good. Therefore, in all circumstances he can be thankful for God's control of his destiny. The early apostles had this one figured out well. As a result, they were recipients of Jesus' promise in John 15:11: "I have told you this so that my joy may be in you and that your joy may be complete."

Yes, Jesus was joyful. He had complete joy during his earthly sojourn, and he is able to provide us with complete joy. But only if we discover how to conform to his will. How can we be certain we are walking in his will for our lives? When we are willing to *joyfully* accept whatever he decides to send our way.

Can we know the will of God for our lives on a daily basis? Certainly—through surrender! Keep in mind that knowing the will of God and being surrendered are inseparably linked. As defined by the passages we have examined, the surrendered heart is characterized by these qualities of humility, total commitment and gratitude. Do these qualities typify your life at the present time? Unless all three are yours, your surrender is suspect and your likelihood of living within God's plans for your life are diminished. Let's surrender and be blessed, confident that we are obeying God's revealed will and living within his customized will for each of our lives!

# Book and Tape Sets
## BY GORDON FERGUSON

All sets include a detailed study guide and four cassette tapes.

### God and History
A survey of the Old Testament with particular emphasis
on how God used the history of Israel to prepare
for the coming of the Messiah.

### The Radical Edge
The dynamic message of the Minor Prophets and its
relevance for Christians today.

### Love One Another
A thorough look at Christian relationships,
including material on discipling.

### Justified: Just As If I'd Never Sinned
A vital study of the Book of Romans and the theme of
justification by grace through faith.

### What About the Holy Spirit?
An in-depth study of a much-neglected subject dealing with
the unique work of the Spirit in the early church
and the power available for us today.

### Powerful Preaching Made Practical
Lessons that will help those who preach as well as those
who lead small discussion groups.

In the US call 1-800-727-8273
From outside the US call 617- 938-7396

OTHER BOOKS FROM
DISCIPLESHIP PUBLICATIONS INTERNATIONAL

**Raising Awesome Kids in Troubled Times**
Sam and Geri Laing

**Mind Change:  The Overcomer's Handbook**
Thomas A. Jones

**She Shall Be Called Woman**
**Volume I: Old Testament Women**
**Volume II: New Testament Women**
edited by Sheila Jones and Linda Brumley

**True and Reasonable**
Douglas Jacoby

THE DAILY POWER SERIES
**Thirty Days at the Foot of the Cross**
**First... the Kingdom**
**Teach Us to Pray**
**To Live Is Christ**

For information about ordering these and
many other resources from DPI call
1-800-727-8273
or from outside the U.S.
617-938-7396
or write to
DPI, One Merrill Street, Woburn, MA 01801

Discipleship Publications International invites you to share with us your response to this book. We want to know what is most helpful to you and what other materials you would find useful.

Write to:
Discipleship Publications International
Attn: Managing Editor
One Merrill Street
Woburn, MA 01801
U.S.A.

Fax to:
1-617-937-3889

Or call toll free:
1-800-727-8273
for current e-mail address.